Madhu Gurung started her career as a journalist and has worked with organizations such as Oxfam, UNIFEM, the BBC World Service Trust and the Bill and Melinda Gates Foundation. Her first book *The Keeper of Memories*, a historical fiction work on the Gorkhas, was shortlisted for the Shakti Bhat First Book Award. *Tibet with My Eyes Closed*, a collection of short stories on Tibetans, is her second book. She lives and works in Dehradun.

TIBET WITH MY EYES CLOSED

Stories

Madhu Gurung

SPEAKING TIGER PUBLISHING PVT. LTD
4381/4, Ansari Road, Daryaganj
New Delhi 110002

First published in paperback by Speaking Tiger 2019

Copyright © Madhu Gurung 2019

ISBN: 978-93-88326-32-2
eISBN: 978-93-89231-05-2

10 9 8 7 6 5 4 3 2 1

All rights reserved.

No part of this publication may be reproduced, transmitted, or stored in a retrieval system, in any form or by any means, electronic, mechanical, photocopying, recording or otherwise, without the prior permission of the publisher.

This book is sold subject to the condition that it shall not, by way of trade or otherwise, be lent, resold, hired out, or otherwise circulated, without the publisher's prior consent, in any form of binding or cover other than that in which it is published.

Contents

Background — ix
Introduction — xiii

BLUE (Sky)
  Zinda — 3
  Sixty-Three — 35
  Jampaling — 58

WHITE (Air)
  The Social Entrepreneur — 77
  Mariko — 90

RED (Fire)
  The Medal — 113
  In the Footsteps of Buddha's Warriors — 126

GREEN (Water)
  Kutta Amma — 161
  The Three Nightingales — 179

YELLOW (Earth)
  Tibet with My Eyes Closed — 197
  Amala — 215

Author's Note — 249

The highest art is the art of living an ordinary life
in an extraordinary way.

—*Old Tibetan Saying*

Background

TIBET HAD THREE traditional regions: Amdo, Kham and U-Tsang. The latter was the seat of the Dalai Lama's power.

It was the summer of 1949 when the People's Liberation Army first walked into Tibet's Western region, Amdo, which borders China's Gansu region. Initially polite and helpful, they would distribute food and medicines. But by 1950 they had moved into Tibet's South East region Kham as well, bordering China's Sichuan. Slowly the PLA began asking people to hand over their guns—Tibetan weapons were highly treasured and were status symbols. Tibetans became increasingly suspicious about the PLA's real intentions. Despite being urged by the Dalai Lama to not resist, the Amdowas and the Khampas joined hands and refused to cooperate with the Chinese. That was when the atrocities began—rape, hanging, monks forced at gunpoint to have intercourse, burning, beheading, flaying, and public 'thamzings' or struggles in which the accused were dragged on to raised platforms, humiliated, beaten, and executed.

All of this only added to Tibetan outrage and resistance. In 1956, the PLA retaliated to their unrest by bombing two major monasteries in Kham and killing over 4000 people who had taken shelter there. In 1957, a businessman named Andrug Gompo Tashi from Lithang began to unify resistance. Ingeniously, he proposed to perform 'Tenshug'—a religious long-life ceremony for the Dalai Lama, in which it was announced a golden throne would be offered. Under the guise of gathering donations, he and his men travelled and unified resistance. On 4 July 1957, the Dalai Lama sat on the throne, made of more than 3000 kilos of pure gold and studded with jewels, to great rejoicing. Under Gompo Tashi, on 16 July 1958, the Chushi Gangdruk or Tibet's resistance movement was born in Drikuthang, Lhokha. 'Chushi Gangdruk' is a Tibetan phrase which means 'Land of Four Rivers and Six Ranges'—a traditional name given to the Eastern Tibetan region of Kham. It is here that the four rivers Salween, Mekong, Yangtze and Yarlung, all arising from the Tibetan plateau, pass through six parallel ranges of mountains that form their watershed.

The Chushi Gangdruk had their own flag on a backdrop of flaming yellow, which was the colour of Buddhism, protecting their religion against the onslaught of the Gyamar (Red Chinese). The flag has two crossed swords—one a flaming sword of Manjushree (a Bodhisattva of wisdom) to slay the ignorance of communism, and the other sword which was commonly used by all Tibetans to signify bravery. The Chushi Gangdruk fought in an age-old tribal way and were no match to the well-equipped Gyamar. That was when Gompo Tashi contacted Gyalo Thondup, the second older brother of the Dalai Lama, who in turn contacted the CIA. The Americans, who had been keen on finding ways to put a stop to communism, agreed to train the men of Chushi Gangdruk. They called the clandestine operation the ST Circus, also known as the Shadow Circus. The first group of six Khampas were trained in guerrilla warfare and radio communications in the Pacific island of Saipan. The second lot were trained in Camp Hale, a former Second World War Camp base in Colorado, USA. Meanwhile, the Tibetan resistance within Tibet continued to clash with the Gyamar.

By March 1959 the Dalai Lama had finished his final Buddhist examination and was invited by the Chinese General to attend a theatrical performance, but with very clear instructions to come without his retinue of bodyguards. The news spread like wildfire and thousands of people thronged Norbulingka, the summer palace of the Dalai Lama, forming a human shield to protect him with their bodies and stop him from leaving the palace.

The Chinese were furious at the Dalai Lama for not accepting their invitation, and at their own inability to control the explosive situation that prevailed. When two Chinese shells exploded in the compound of the Norbulingka palace, the Dalai Lama consulted the state oracle and was advised to flee. On 17 March 1959, the Dalai Lama, along with his family and closest aides, fled Tibet.

The Chushi Gangdruk too left Tibet to set up a guerrilla camp in the windswept mountain crags of Mustang in Western Nepal by early 1960. From there they would cross over into Tibet and conduct raids on the Gyamar forces. The India-China War of 1962 resulted in the creation of an elite force that enlisted Tibetans, which was joined by many young men to defend the borders of India instead of fighting for their homeland. Meanwhile, American interest in the Tibetan cause began waning with the end of the Cold War and the election of President Nixon in 1968. That was when the Americans started their rapprochement with the Chinese, during which one of the first demands of China was for the Americans to withdraw support to the Tibetan warriors. The Americans withdrew swiftly but the Tibetans carried on. But wrecked by internal strife and without international support for their cause, by 1974 the resistance movement was over.

In sixty years of living in India, the Dalai Lama has propagated Tibetan Buddhism and has been recognized as an Apostle of Peace. He has also proposed the Middle Way as a solution to the sixty years of Chinese occupation of their homeland. The Middle Way asks only for the autonomy of Tibetans in Tibet. This continues to be unacceptable to China.

Introduction

THE FLAG OF a nation is its soul.

Prayer flags of five colours are synonymous with Tibetan Buddhism. There are many legends attached to these flags. There is one legend which attributes the origin of the prayer flags to Gautam Buddha himself, whose prayers were written and carried by Indian bhikshus as his banner and commitment to ahimsa. Another legend says that cloth prayer flags existed much before the advent of Buddhism in Tibet and were used by the Bon shamanistic religion. The Buddhists believe that the flags promote peace, compassion, strength and wisdom, with the winds carrying the goodwill and blessings of the mantras pervading across all spaces to bless each sentient being. Even as they fade from exposure to the elements of nature, they become a permanent part of the universe.

The five colours represent the five elements. Blue symbolizes the sky and space. White symbolizes the air and wind. Red symbolizes fire. Green symbolizes water. Yellow symbolizes the earth.

Each of the stories I tell you today epitomizes one core element of the prayer flags—space, wind, fire, water, and earth. That is how I have grouped the stories, for they have some element of that colour woven into their background.

The Blue section stories *Zinda, Sixty-Three* and *Jampaling* are stitched on to the sky that stretches all the way to their homeland—the place where they have laid down their hearts. In their new home they came not as refugees who flee natural disasters, but as what the Dalai Lama calls 'Tsenjol-wa'—people who were forced to flee. The sky in their new home is never quite the same.

The winds of change sweep through the next section, White, through the stories of young Tibetans born and brought up in India. Whatever they know about their Tibetan-ness is from what they have heard and learnt from the community. But they cannot help picking up on subtle nuances of change in thinking, attitude and assimilation to carve out their own paths and identities.

The Red section signifies fire. The turning point in Tibetan history came with the rule of Songsten Gompo, who by around 640 CE managed to get together Tibet's warring clans to harness their power outwards, alongside his warriors who painted their faces red and attacked with the fierce war cry of *ki ki so so lha gyalo!*, or 'May the God be Victorious,' managing to capture significant parts of China. As the first of the dharma kings, he is responsible for getting Buddhism into Tibet. After him, in the winter of 763 CE, a victorious Tibetan army marched into Chang'an (Xi'an), China's great Tang empire that controlled the trading Silk Route. But centuries later, by 1959, things had changed. Chinese occupation of Tibet forced the Tibetans to flee their homeland. The only fire

Introduction

left was the clandestine and unfeted guerrilla wars that the Tibetans fought for their homeland. From the windswept Mustang plateau in Nepal that stands out as a red band of raw courage, the Tibetans took on the world's largest army, the PLA, from 1960 to 1974. In the milieu of the peaceful Middle Way advocated by His Holiness the Dalai Lama, the only wars the Tibetans silently participated in were not for their own homeland, but for their adopted country India.

There is an old Tibetan proverb: 'Words are mere bubbles in water, deeds are drops of gold'. The nature of water is that nobody can stop the waves, but the stories in the Green section, *Kutta Amma* and *The Three Nightingales*, depict learning to surf the tide. An old woman finds solace in looking after the neglected stray dogs of Dehradun. In Dharamshala, three women rekindle their childhood friendship in singing ancient songs passed on from generations, their voices rising and falling like rippling waters, playful wind playing hide-and-seek on a sweeping plateau to celebrate and echo in their new land.

Mother Earth epitomizes the last colour Yellow, and is the final element of the Tibetan prayer flag. Like the earth, it is all-giving; like a mother it gives birth, nurtures and sets you on your journey of possibilities. It is for Mother Earth that you yearn, whom you return to in your dreams. The two stories *Tibet with My Eyes Closed* and *Amala* epitomize that very essence.

These are true stories of ordinary Tibetans who have lived ordinary lives in extraordinary times of losing a homeland forever. They live that loss every day even as they build new dreams. There is an old Tibetan saying: 'If I tell you my dream, you might forget it. If I act on my dream, perhaps you will remember it, but if I involve you—it becomes your dream too.'

I hope their stories touch your dreams...

BLUE
Sky

Zinda

His dreams were always the same.

The familiar feeling of fear started at the pit of his stomach and gripped his guts in a clammy feeling of helplessness. The bone-chilling mountain wind whipped at his fur-lined ear flaps. The horse bridle jingled as heavily armed, raw-boned Khampas pulled the harnesses and led them up the steep mountain in waist-deep snow, their misty breath stolen and carried away by the howling winds through the inky night. The only sounds, besides the hooves and jangle of bridles, were tired coughs as the caravan moved in the dead of night.

He sat in front of his Aunt Lhamo on a black horse, and she bundled him as best as she could, shielding him with her body. He looked up and saw his father riding in front just behind his Uncle, the Penda Rinpoche. Behind them was a retinue of thirty-five monks and servants. The caravan turned a stoop, and they got down to rest a while. Aunt Lhamo reached out, put a stone over a stone and whispered, 'Lha Gyalo'—Victory to the Gods.

She held one out for him to touch and then turned to place it over her own. 'We will come back Sangay... soon, very soon.' He opened his mouth, his tears turning to ice as he whispered, 'Aamo,' the bewildered cry of a five-year-old for the mother they had left behind to look after the old grandparents in Zinda, their native village in Kham.

Lhamo hugged him and whispered fiercely as if promising herself, 'We will come back for her, I promise. Soon, very soon.' The sound of gunfire galvanized them into action as men pulled at the harnesses. Sangay felt his breath catch in his throat. Fear enveloped him as if he had been pushed off a cliff and was flying through terrifying darkness with no end in sight. His scream congealed in his throat, he had difficulty breathing the cold rarified mountain air that still surrounded him.

He woke up sweating, his heart thudding, eyes dilated in fear.

Decades had passed, yet the same persistent dream—haunting in its stark reality—returned from time to time to resurrect forgotten panic and fear. It was like tearing at scabs that had formed over deep wounds, making him bleed all over again. He could no longer distinguish the five-year-old boy from the twenty-eight-year-old man he had become. The dream blurred reality.

He reached for a drink of water, his eyes still riveted on the path they had taken so many years ago. The Jamas, the Chinese, were everywhere. They came up like wild mushrooms that inundated the meadows in the spring. Sangay always associated the Jamas with wild mushrooms: pretty to look at, but poisonous. Dressed in beige Chinese collared mufti, the senior officers powdered their faces white. They kept telling everyone that the rich and the monks had taken from the peasants and built a fortune.

Their brand of communism, they said, would make everyone equal.

He remembered his mother's fear as she held him, shielding him with her body while she nursed his one-year-old brother, Tsungma. The Chinese were outside their home, talking to his grandfather. While their leader spoke to his grandfather the other men were running their eyes over their home, the sweeping land resplendent with the ripening barley crop and the rolling meadows of lazily grazing yaks and sheep. Their eyes were everywhere as if assessing their worth.

His grandfather, Chamchu Sangpo, was the richest man in the village of Zinda. He was tall with long hair that he wore in a braid entwined with red silk that reached below his waist. Big turquoise earrings studded in gold adorned his ears and glinted in the sun. When he smiled, it was as if the sun was shimmering over the Drichu river that frolicked by their land and where they would bathe, play and fish. In his dark chuba and embroidered knee-length boots, he cut a dapper figure. He had been born rich, with acres and acres of cultivated fields and wild pastures, as far as the eye could see, for his cattle and horses to graze on. His hard work had increased his fortune manifold. Everyone looked up to him.

Their three-storeyed home was large and housed the stables on the ground floor along with the servants' quarters. The first floor had a large kitchen with an iron hearth where the fires never stopped burning. Next to it was his parents' room and a large store. The top floor was reserved for the family altar and their grandfather's room.

The surrounding meadows had shelters and pens built for hundreds of yaks and sheep. Every Losar, his grandfather opened up their home for four days of feasting for everyone from their village and the neighbouring villages as well.

Every six months his father, Zenu Loden or Zenga as he was known to everyone, and his grandfather along with a small army of servants and other traders would herd hundreds of horses, yaks and sheep along with mules carrying provisions—butter, tea, sheepskin and wool— and head to Lhasa for trade. They were mounted on stout ponies and carried guns and swords to protect their caravan from dacoits on the way. It would be an arduous journey, over the vast barren plateau and treacherous snow-peaked mountain passes, taking over six months to reach their destination. Most of their goods were bought by the monasteries and traders from Nepal. His grandfather also dealt in amber and turquoise, which fetched a high price. At times they even travelled as far away as Kalimpong in India and brought back many different pots and cooking utensils for feasts.

When the men returned after months from such a sojourn, smelling of Lhasa and trading halts and full of tales of new things they had witnessed, they would regale everyone with endless stories that took many days to recount by the warm kitchen hearth. His mother and grandmother and a horde of servants would bustle around cooking over the large iron stove. It was the best time for the family. Sangay clung to their words as they painted a distant world of alien people. Like most Tibetans, he too believed that beyond China, Nepal and India from where the traders came, they were surrounded by an endless ocean.

But the one story that stuck in Sangay's head was about his grandfather's visit to Drikuthang, in Lhokha, on their way from Lhasa. Although he could not understand too well, from subdued expressions and lowered voices he had heard his grandfather say that the Tibetans had started a resistance movement, Chushi Gangdruk, taking on the original name of Kham and Amdo—Four Rivers and Six Ranges. Already his favourite uncle Palden, his father's first cousin, had secretly left home to gather men for the cause. He was a hulk of a man, broad-chested and full of vigour. His grandfather said Palden and other Tibetan warriors were the defenders of Tibet and Buddhism against the Jamas.

Just hearing them made Sangay impatient to grow up. 'When will I join Chushi Gangdruk, Apa?' he had questioned his father, and a hush had fallen among adult conversation. It was his grandfather who had pulled him to his knee and said, 'When you are thirteen and will be of some use to them. Till then, concentrate on becoming a good rider and a good marksman. If I cannot give my two sons to the cause I can give my grandson.' It had made Sangay feel important but his mother had looked stricken. Even his father was strangely silent.

As the months passed more Chinese appeared. There were also snatches of conversation of ongoing wars—some days tilted in the Tibetans' favor, at other times won by the Chinese. Two nights before Losar, Sangay woke up hearing some people talking. He walked into the kitchen to find silent unkempt men sitting around the fire eating voraciously, their guns and swords heaped on the mud-washed floor. Their leader and his grandfather were having a serious conversation while his father listened intently. The men left as silently as they had come, carrying away over a hundred of grandfather's horses, laden with tents and provisions. He watched as the mist enveloped them in its silver shroud.

Losar came and went with the same fervour, but he could see that his grandfather, the men, and even the servants were preoccupied. There was little dancing and horse racing, instead men huddled together talking intently. Something was very wrong. Sangay could feel it. Their servant Chogu never left him alone, and there was something watchful in his manner. Even grandfather and his father constantly surveyed the horizon as if waiting for something to happen.

The Chinese came a few days after the festivities. They forced everyone out of their homes—men, women, children. This time they were rough, grim-faced, their guns menacing. They left carrying away one man from each household. Uncle Palden stepped out willingly when they asked who would accompany them from Sangay's family, even before grandfather could say a word.

The moment the Chinese left, the men of their household began tersely conferring in the stables. His mother took him to the kitchen to feed him. He was sleeping when he woke up to his mother's gentle touch. He looked up to see his father fully dressed in his outdoor clothes. He was holding his warm coat and fur-lined cap.

But it was his Aunt Lhamo, his father's younger sister, a nun at the nearby nunnery, who dressed him up. She pulled on his yak fur-lined coat, kissed him softly, and said, 'We are going to meet your uncle, the Penda Rinpoche in Zefu.' Aunt Lhamo was so pretty that despite shaving off her long hair she still appeared just like the angels that adorned the walls of the monastery. Sangay sat up fully awake, excitement dancing in his eyes. He loved his father's solemn elder brother who was always immersed in prayers, or meeting the hordes of people who came for his guidance and blessings.

He ran downstairs to see the whole family had assembled there. Already the mules had been loaded.

'Don't trouble father or Aunt Lhamo too much. Be good,' his mother said, sitting on her haunches. Her eyes were troubled. She held him tight and touched his face tenderly, kissing his forehead. He was too excited to hug her back. His grandmother too kissed his forehead, while rocking his younger brother, Tsungma, who had fallen asleep. As they moved to the horses, his grandfather put him on the saddle in front of his father and patted him on his head. 'We will see you soon,' he said as he stepped away, looking solemn as they turned the horses and left their homestead.

Zefu was just an hour's ride, past rolling alpine meadows and white cotton clouds that raced with them. The Penda Rinpoche was resting after lunch when they reached him. He too had heard growing rumblings of the Chinese rounding up people and taking them away to prison and labour camps. The two brothers decided to move up to

Lhasa and return once things had calmed down. They left on horses two days later, carrying food, provisions and a train of people who attended to the Rinpoche.

Every morning they would ride out and by late afternoon pitch their tents, usually by a flowing stream or river. The men would guard the camp with their kedun, fierce fighting swords, and guns. After a night's rest they would start out again. Everyone in Kham carried guns and swords and the men encouraged Sangay to hold a kedun on his own, grunting approval when he held one steadily. It was an exciting time for Sangay who had never been on such a long trip. Every day was an adventure, riding the vast wind-swept plateau. At night, by the fire, the men always talked about the Jamas, the way they had steadily entered Kham and Amdo in growing numbers. Now they were killing Tibetans and imprisoning them at will, in a bid to take over their land.

The mornings were filled with new sights, people and travel such that Sangay seldom remembered his mother—but at night by the camp fire, when he was tucked in his bed, he would ask for his Aamo. Instead Aunt Lhamo would always have lots of stories to tell him as she lay down beside him. They were the stories she had heard as a child herself. The ones he loved best were those of fierce ancestors with red painted faces, who fought on swift horses, forcing their enemies to quake and flee in fear, creating a Tibetan empire inside China's heartland and trading routes right into Mongolia and the Turkish empire.

On nights when she did not tell stories she would point

out the stars, naming all the brilliant heavenly bodies that dotted the inky sky. Wrapped in warm fur, he would hear her till sleep overcame him.

A week into their travel they began noticing more caravans which were also travelling to Lhasa. Every day they grew in number; it was as if entire villages were moving. It took over forty days to reach Lhasa. To everyone's surprise, the Jamas were already there. There were large Chinese camps, heavily cordoned and armed with tanks and machine guns. There was a palpable sense of fear that enveloped the streets, as if they were waiting for lightning to strike and could smell the approaching rain. They learnt that the Dalai Lama was in Norbulingka, his summer palace.

The two brothers decided to travel to the Ngor monastery, the seat of the Penda Rinpoche. They had been on the move for almost two months and they hoped they could finally rest in Ngor.

Ngor was peaceful. It was the beginning of March 1959 and the air was redolent with the coming of spring. It was the best time to be travelling in Tibet, his father said, as they went to sleep. They woke up to the sounds of explosions, and the earth shaking as if there was an earthquake. This was followed in quick succession by a relentlessly aggressive pounding. It was still dark outside. Everyone ran to the windows and the courtyard—a sea of fearful monks, some mumbling prayers for protection, the younger ones crying out at each explosion.

Some older monks climbed the monastery's roof as more explosions sounded. Someone shouted, 'Bombs are falling from the sky.' But it was a voice that yelled, 'Lhasa is burning. I can see fire and black smoke enveloping Lhasa,' that started a fearful moaning. Men scrambled out to the open courtyard to see what was happening. The unremitting bombing continued, compounding fear and uncertainty.

At daybreak some men came riding into the monastery. They carried news that the Dalai Lama had fled Tibet a day earlier and was heading for India. Everyone was in a state of panic. The Chinese were bombing all Tibetan landmarks—Norbulingka, even the Potala palace and Sera monastery. Thousands had died as they clashed with the Chinese army. The Chinese were killing everyone Tibetan. As the day progressed, there was a steady stream of fleeing people and by sunset they had turned into a silent fearful sea of humanity. They carried with them the urgency and fear that enveloped the very air they were breathing, contaminating everyone they passed on the route to escape.

The two brothers decided they would go to India and return home once everything calmed down. The Penda Rinpoche gave orders for his monks to head for India. Travelling in groups, they packed what little they could and left Ngor. Their route was through the high mountain passes. In the high mountains Sangay felt giddy and unwell, and the blinding glare of the snow made his eyes water. His father forced him to suck on ice to stay hydrated. The air was thin and the going fraught with danger as the Chinese were bombing the fleeing Tibetans from the air as well. Fear was their constant enemy. Whenever the air raids would start, they would hide in snowy stoops. Sangay would cry for Aamo, only to be told they would go home as soon as the Jamas left their homeland.

After fourteen days of trampling up high mountain passes, pursued by the Chinese army, their party finally arrived at Lachen Lachung in Sikkim. Among thousands of milling Tibetans entering Sikkim, they found some relatives from Zinda. It was a tearful meeting, an outpouring of grief and stories of loss; how the Chinese had overrun the village, commandeering homes and farmlands of the landlords. They hung on to every word, holding their breaths, afraid to ask about Aamo and the grandparents. They were told that all the landowners and their families were either killed or sent to labour camps. His father was silent for days after that. Sangay instinctively knew he was not to ever question him about home. Deep down he knew his mother, brother and grandparents were all dead. He found answers in his father's shadowed eyes and long silences.

Everything about India was strange—the language, the food and the people. Sangay got ill just eating the Indian diet of dal bhaat. Thousands around them, bred on roasted tsampa and butter and meat, were getting sick and dying like flies. His father sold some silver coins. Each coin fetched them five rupees and that allowed them to buy food and other necessities. They hired a bare, cold room which everyone camped in. They were better off than thousands who lived under tarpaulins or slept under the open sky to be hired in 'road gangs', which cleared forests and tarred roads. Bewilderment and acute hopelessness pervaded the day-to-day existence of all Tibetans.

For a year they lived on the fringes of the Sikkim border. His father took up buying wool, travelling to small bastis and selling it. They survived with whatever they had, selling their silver. Aunt Lhamo and some of the servants began working as labour. Sangay found himself with other children, playing with stones and squatting in the dust, grimy and with matted hair. Just surviving each day kept them occupied, making them think less and less of Tibet.

A year later they moved to Darjeeling where a large number of people were settling. They stayed by an open ground on the hill that overlooked a majestic blue-domed palace. His father's wool business did better, as many Tibetan women had learnt how to use knitting needles and make sweaters. Hand-knit sweaters were highly sought after, a fashion statement which fetched a good amount. Aunt Lhamo made the first sweater for Sangay. It was sky blue—'just like the sky over Zinda,' she said, with tears in her eyes.

He was eight when the 1962 Indo-China war broke out. When the war ended, the Penda Rinpoche expressed a desire to move to a place called Dehradun where the Sakya king, Sakya Trizin, was heading. They had heard the Dalai Lama was in Dharamshala and had put together settlements for Tibetans to live in. Living together meant collective strength.

They travelled for seven days by train, passing arid plains and meandering rivers, and many jostling stations of people who heaved and squeezed into the berths they had paid for. They had not been allowed to carry their luggage in the coach. Everything they owned, precious gold and silver prayer-ware studded with jewels, was put in gunny bags and loaded haphazardly on to a goods train. It took over a month to reach Dehradun, by which time they had almost given up hope. Luckily all the goods were intact.

In tree-lined Rajpur, a quiet suburb of Dehradun by the blue hills of Mussoorie, they rebuilt their lives in an old British-style bungalow. Aunt Lhamo joined a nunnery started by the Sakya Trizin and lived in the adjacent compound of the Penda Rinpoche. The Rinpoche spent most of his time in prayers and in aiding his followers. Aunt Lhamo would visit them once a month. She was the closest to a mother now for Sangay. His father had become a man of few words. When he was home, he would sit in his room reading the Rinpoche's religious texts. It left Sangay very much alone. With each passing year the dream of returning to Tibet became more distant. His father would often say there was nothing to go back to. Their land was now China's land. Their life was where the Dalai Lama lived and they were lucky they had him to show them how to build a new life.

To earn a livelihood, his father started a sweater business. Travelling to Ludhiana, an industrial town in Punjab, at the start of autumn along with other Tibetans, he would return with sack-loads of sweaters in rainbow hues. Then he would start a gypsy salesman existence. Travelling across Indian towns—Bombay, Bhopal, Patna, Gaya, Dehradun, Calcutta, Darjeeling—and onwards to tourist destinations during winters to sell sweaters. He and his friends would sit on makeshift tarpaulins near crowded markets and lay out their wares. They learnt to bargain in Hindi.

His father cut off his long hair; the long braid threaded in red lay wrapped in a cloth at the bottom of his tin trunk, the last remnants of a life from Tibet. Sangay started school. Shy and reticent, along with other Tibetan boys his age, he began learning English. Very often he and his Tibetan friends were mistaken for Gorkhas or for Nagas. When he insisted he was Tibetan, he encountered sniggers. No one had heard about Tibet. He realized that for most Indians, the Tibetans were the 'nowhere' people who existed on the fringes of India's goodwill. However, beyond the classrooms in the football field, he found himself and could let go of his pent-up pain.

He missed his mother most during Losar and on his birthdays. His father made it a point to be home for him. Her loss was a shadow between them. As he grew older, his father would talk of Tibet, recalling wistfully all the things he had done as a boy, his wedding and how he felt as he saw Sangay's little face for the first time. Then he would turn angry and belligerent about what the Chinese had done to their homeland. What little news they got of Tibet was of oppression and the ruthless destruction of everything Tibetan. Gradually, with a resigned heart, he began saying, 'Why cling to the soil, when our souls are with us…'

During school vacations Sangay went travelling with his father, helping him put up stalls and sell sweaters, caps, socks and mittens. When he finished school, he began to work full time.

Along with a friend Sangay travelled to Kalimpong and Chennai, bought curios and brassware and set up a shop in Leh, which was booming as a tourist destination. For six months, during the summer tourist season, he lived in Leh, and the other six months he helped his father in his sweater business. It was difficult but he was able to straddle both worlds. He wanted his father to stop working, as years of travel and eating in indifferent dhabas had affected his health. But Sangay also realized that the business was his father's only window to the world.

One autumn when he returned from Leh, his father insisted that they visit a family living nearby. Sangay went along, only to realize his father had been match-making. Dikyi was a beautiful young woman whose parents too were from Kham. It was a match the Penda Rinpoche had blessed. Sangay's only protest was he was just twenty-four and still too young to get married.

'I married when I was twenty and your mother was just fourteen, a cheeky girl with twinkling eyes,' his father had retorted, choking up as he walked away. When wedding preparations got underway, he would sit on his favourite chair and tell Sangay about the red chuba trimmed with fur that his mother had worn for their wedding, her traditional turquoise and amber headgear and other finery. He remembered how they had danced and feasted for days. It was the longest his father had spoken about his mother. For the first time since they came to India, they had something to celebrate.

Dikyi brought happiness in their lives. His father was glad to hear them banter and laugh at small things. He would smile when Dikyi served him food and included him in the jokes they shared. The young couple had three children in quick succession. 'Each child makes my blood grow and my old heart stronger and gives me a reason to live long,' the older man said, his eyes diamond bright.

Then the Penda Rinpoche died in his sleep. His death was like severing the last familiar link with Tibet. A repository of all Tibetan learning, he had been their guide and mentor. His father said the Rinpoche had arranged the wedding as he had a premonition of death. The children and Dikyi made his loss easier to bear.

For years they had been paying for a small home in a Tibetan colony that the Dalai Lama had named Dekyiling—the place where happiness and peace prevails. Ironically it was ready after Penda Rinpoche's death. The family shifted into their new home, stringing prayer flags from their rooftop that had been blessed by the monastery next door. Dekyiling was a self-sufficient Tibetan colony, and on weekends and festivals Aunt Lhamo would come and live with them.

Dikyi had taken to volunteering at the weaving centre's office. She came home one evening with news that the Chinese government had opened up Tibet and was issuing visas to any Tibetan wanting to visit. It was March 1980, and both Sangay and his father were scornful about the Chinese government's olive branch. Their skepticism was shared by most Tibetans.

Once the children came along, both Dikyi and Sangay

insisted that his father had slogged enough and it was now his turn to be taken care of. Zenga agreed and only on some Sundays would he take over the small stall they had at the Parade Ground, nicknamed the Tibetan market, so that Sangay and his family could have an outing. Their home in Dekyiling resounded with the happy noises of children growing up. The moment Sangay returned home he would be greeted with an all-enveloping warmth. It was a perfect life.

The approaching winter marked the sweater business booming as tourists heading for Mussoorie and beyond bought woollies. Sundays were particularly busy. Sangay was tired when he came home that Sunday and let himself in. There was a visitor, a man sitting with his father. 'Sangay,' the man rose and enveloped him in a bear hug.

'Tenzin?' Sangay cried, greeting his childhood neighbour from Kham. The two had been best buddies, racing around the open meadows together. Sangay thumped his friend on his back. He was seeing him after years, as he lived and worked in distant Kathmandu.

'What a pleasant surprise,' Sangay said, grinning at his friend. He turned to his father with a smile and froze. His father appeared carved out of burnt wood, his eyes desolate and etched with immense pain. The letter in his hand had been folded and unfolded many times over.

'Apa, what's wrong?' Sangay asked in alarm. Wordlessly his father handed him the letter he was holding.

It was in Tibetan. Sangay sped through it and came to the lines, '...I am alive. Yes, both me and Tsungma are alive. Not a single day has passed when I have not prayed that God keeps Sangay and you alive and well.'

'Your mother and your brother have been alive all these years,' his father said, his voice cracking, trailing into silence. Sangay reached for his father instinctively. It was the first time in years that they had embraced like this in shared pain. His father keeled over and cried in huge mournful sobs as if his stout mountain heart was breaking. Sangay cried for all the barren years of growing up without a mother. They cried for all the lost years of never knowing. Each thought was a swirling whirlpool of loss.

They stayed that way for a long time. Dikyi kept the children at bay and got them tea. They clung to each word that Tenzin spoke about his trip to Tibet to look for his parents back in Kham. His father had been publicly executed for trying to escape from Kham. His mother survived and stayed in Zinda with relatives.

Tenzin had made it to Zinda to a rousing welcome from the entire village. News of his arrival spread wide. Almost a week later he had a visitor who came carrying a gift of freshly made butter. 'It was your mother. She blessed me and hesitatingly asked if I knew if Zenga Loden and Sangay were alive.

'I told her that you both were alive and well. I had to tell her several times for her to believe me. I also told her that you thought she was dead. Your mother cried a lot. She asked me again and again to describe you both, even your wife, Dikyi. She is well and your younger brother Tsungma is a successful businessman. But they are the only ones from your family who are now alive.' Everything Tenzin said moved them to more tears.

Shortly after, Tenzin stood up to go. He was determined to leave, despite Sangay's insistence for him to stay. 'Brother, I have just come from Tibet and my passport has a Chinese stamp. The Indian government is very suspicious of all such coming and going. I don't want my coming here to put your family under a cloud. I too might get arrested on the smallest suspicion, although I have done no wrong.' Sangay nodded; he had never thought of such a thing but knew that as refugees in exile they always had to be on the right side of the law.

He walked his friend to the waiting taxi that would take him straight to Delhi airport. 'Sangay, you are lucky your mother and brother are alive—you must visit them in Tibet. Your mother is old and life is fragile, don't keep her waiting too long.'

Everyone from the neighbourhood descended on them, eager to hear their miracle. Aunt Lhamo also came. She was the one who consoled his father and him, smiling through her tears.

That night the dream was back. He woke up with a start as he saw himself hurtling down the snow-capped peaks of the high Himalayan pass, his scream leaving him breathless.

He stood up and padded to his father's room. His father was sitting up in his bed, telling his beads. He was still holding mother's letter in his hand.

The next day he broached the topic that now consumed him. 'Apa, I shall travel to Zinda. Now that we know mother is alive, I have to go to her.' His father shook his head, 'The Jamas will never leave you, you won't be able to come back. I can't live without you also.'

They had their first argument and it escalated every time he broached the subject. It was almost three months later when his father relented, giving in to Sangay's determination that he needed to go to his mother as she was waiting for him. Dikyi helped him garner the finances he needed, assuring him that she would take care of the family while he was gone. A whole year later, when he had enough money, he applied for a visa.

It was a long exhausting wait while the Chinese authorities verified his mother and brother's existence in Kham, before allowing him a travel permit. His father cried when he left home, standing by the door, a cane in hand. It struck Sangay as the taxi turned the hill road and headed for the dusty plains that he had never seen his father look so vulnerable.

He took the cheapest route to Tibet, flying into Kathmandu and from there along with some twenty other Tibetans travelling by road to Tatopani, the last Nepali border post. Crossing the Chinese border police post, they climbed a truck going to Lhasa. Everyone was silently taking in the journey. Small towns came and they recognized names like Nyelam and Shigatse where they stopped for food. The Chinese truck they travelled in was in poor condition and would break down often. Dust was their constant companion, swirling on the unmetalled road and settling on their clothes and person.

It was harvest season and the fields were full of Tibetans cutting the crop. With a shock they saw their poor condition. Everyone was sunburnt, their hands and feet had cuts and bruises from constant labour and their clothes were all patched. The children looked thin and malnourished.

At nightfall Sangay and his group stopped at a guest house where they were welcomed by Tibetans wearing the chuba and subjected to a monologue about the progress made under Chinese rule in Tibet. All welcomes to guest houses were the same. Often the rooms were in darkness as there was no electricity. They tried buying candles in the next town but drew a blank as there were none. Even among themselves the group did not speak about all that they were witnessing, afraid they would be prosecuted or arrested. Very often someone in the group would be crying silently or praying.

Four days later the truck reached Lhasa and someone pointed to the Potala palace. They had heard that it had been bombed in 1959 by the Chinese. But it appeared intact and they dismounted and kissed the ground, promising to circumambulate its circumference before leaving Tibet.

It didn't feel like home, but he had reached his homeland.

From Lhasa the group of twenty scattered. Sangay was left with a fellow Tibetan man and his quiet wife who were also heading for Kham. The Chinese truck that took them to Siling was dilapidated and did not have headlights; they shacked up in guest rooms at night. At each guest house the monologue of the greatness of the Chinese government followed them. It took a week of travel through the desolate plateau to reach Siling. The town stores had barely anything they could buy. They began noticing that most Tibetans did not wear a chuba. They learnt that everything was rationed, even cloth, and there was never enough for making a chuba. Anyone Sangay spoke to would keep looking over their shoulder to see if any Chinese were listening.

There was no bus available for Chengdu, so they took a lift from a truck heading there with sacks of barley. It was cold sitting atop the open truck. When they stopped for a meal, the driver softly asked them if they had met His Holiness the Dalai Lama.

'Once, when he came to bless our colony in Dehradun in India. We were lucky to be in his presence,' Sangay said. The driver sat desolate, tears flooding his eyes. His helper, a man with a pronounced limp, also cried when he heard Sangay talk about His Holiness.

Quietly the driver spoke about the constant fear and troubles the Tibetans lived with. 'I am lucky I can drive. My brother was put to work as a labourer making roads and bridges. He had to carry huge boulders the whole day, and when his back got sores he was bandaged and sent back to work without rest. A year ago he broke his leg from a fall. Forget medicines, he was not given food. He would have died of starvation if I had not taken him home from the camp. When he was better I began teaching him how to drive. That's how we go around in the truck together, he is the second driver and mechanic.

'We have been told we Tibetans have too many children and now we should control the number of children to just two. Food coupons are severely rationed and there is always a shortage of food,' he said.

They stopped for the night at Chekudo town, just three hours from Zinda. Sangay had been on the road for over two weary weeks.

He woke up to streaming sunshine and a brilliant blue sky. He had a quick wash and got ready. There was a knock on the door. A young man in his early twenties stood before him, his eyes hesitant.

He bowed low in the Chinese style and asked, 'Aro?'

'Tsungma,' Sangay whispered. The young man nodded, his eyes filling up as he rushed headlong into his brother's embrace. Twenty-three years melted away as Sangay embraced the tall fair stranger.

The wind raced with them. The two men were on horses that Tsungma had brought with him. Sangay urged his horse forward; he hadn't ridden a horse since leaving Tibet but instinctively remembered how to ride. They rode through the vast alpine meadow, the smell of yak dung assailing his senses. He could see a herd of yaks and sheep grazing at a distance. They slowed to a trot. Sangay drank in the scene, and for the first time since entering Tibet he felt that he was home. At a distance he could see a number of Ba or black yak skin tents, with smoke curling from a couple of them. They had been spotted and people were running towards them. They dismounted, leaving their horses tethered to trees. Sangay could see a whole row of women dressed in dark chubas. Some were carrying white khatas. They were all weeping.

Which one was his mother? He stood there uncertain, his heart thudding in nervousness.

Tsungma took his hand and gently led him to a grey-haired woman with fair skin and tears streaming down her cheeks.

'Aamo,' he said not knowing what to do. With a sob she put her arms around him, holding him tight, her cries like an animal in pain. Sangay held her, crying bitterly as if he would never let her go. She smelt of freshly churned butter and crushed grass.

She ran her calloused hands over his face, her nails broken and lined with dirt beneath. She caressed his face tenderly as if trying to see traces of the child she had sent away. She kissed his forehead just as she had done when they parted.

'My child, my son,' she cried brokenly, over and over again as she held him, her hands soothing his back as if wiping the shadows that had separated them.

The women surrounded them, hugging and touching him.

He had finally come home.

His mother's home, he realized, was a tent. She and her maternal family lived as nomads. Tsungma was already married and lived separately. The yaks and sheep were his mother's only worldly possessions. It was a hard existence. Waking up at four in the morning, she would kindle her kitchen fire for her first cup of butter tea and then fetch water, in a sloshing bucket made of the yak stomach, from the river. She would make several trips and then cook herself a small meal. Setting out after her herd of grazing yaks and sheep, she would spend the whole day in the sun. Before sundown she would herd them back and milk them, storing the milk in wooden pails. It was hard to see his mother work this way, without any rest and comfort. As a young woman she had been attended to by an army of servants.

The day he saw her churning butter made him desperate. Using a traditional wooden churn, she went on swishing the swirling cream for hours till it finally yielded butter. She stood up stiff and bent from all the churning. The butter was sold in the local market and the money used to buy her stock of tsampa and other basics. Restless, the next day he went to Chekudo and returned with a Chinese-made professional butter-maker that ran on chargeable battery. It cost him 800 yuan which was 8200 rupees. It ate into his pocket but was worth every bit. When they made butter again, it was the machine that worked and not his mother.

If he tried to help her with her work, she would shoo him away and tell him to rest, saying she didn't mind working. Slowly, from strangers they hesitantly stepped into the roles of mother and son, still unsure of boundaries but with gratitude that life had given them a second chance. He would catch her several times looking at him when she thought he wasn't aware, with an enormous love that made his breath catch in his throat.

His brother went home after a week as he had business to attend to and a family that was waiting. Together he and his mother talked endlessly. She told him about how the Chinese had come home the very day after they had left. 'They stormed the house searching for all the menfolk. The same Chinese officer who had been so polite was cold and ruthless. The soldiers hit your grandfather with rifle butts when he asked them to leave. They dragged him and flung him out of the house. He was bleeding and in pain when we ran to help him up. They told the servants, "These people have made a fortune on your backs, if you assist them it will be death or a labour camp, you choose." We were told that the house and land no longer belonged to us. It was the property of the Chinese government.'

That night the family spent cold and hungry in the yak pen. From then on, the pen was their home. The Chinese fed them boiled barley husk with dried beetroot twice a day. It tasted like ditch-water.

His grandfather and mother had to work as labourers on the very farm that had been their family's for generations. His grandmother was told to look after a number of children so their mothers could work. They dug, tilled the land and planted rows of vegetables for the Chinese army. In the winter of 1959, the poor diet and intense labour took a toll on grandfather. He caught dysentery and was unable to work. 'I had nothing to give him, no medicine, no food...' his mother recalled with sadness.

'I begged the Chinese officer for a doctor to see grandfather but he told me there were none. That night your grandfather died. It was September-end. The next morning I went to the supervisor begging for firewood for his cremation. He refused. So I carried your grandfather on my back, with your grandmother helping me, and put him in the river. We watched him float away without any funeral rites or ceremony, just the tears of two women.

'The river took him away, slowly at first, and then rapidly. Your grandmother and I watched him go till we could see him no more.' Her voice cracked and she wiped her eyes with her calloused hands. Sangay held her and cried for his grandfather, remembering the tall man with his long hair braided in red silk and a smile like the sun shimmering over the Drichu river.

'Your grandmother and I survived till 1962 when China went to war with India. The Chinese diverted all their resources to the war front and once again there was an acute shortage of food. Your grandmother died then from starvation. After your grandfather's death she had lost the will to live. I was alone with your brother. Even I was very sick. A woman informed my family in Antho and they came, took me away and nursed me to health. I sold my gold ornaments and bought some yaks and sheep and slowly started all over again.'

'Did you not think of father and me? Of where we were?' Sangay asked.

'Not a day went by that I did not pray that you come back for me and your brother. I prayed that you both stayed safe.'

She clung to every word that Sangay recounted of their journey and what transpired, often asking him to repeat and describe the place, savouring what he recounted, almost as if she was walking alongside and reliving their lives.

'Do you know Aamo, in Hindi, the language spoken by Indians, the name of our village—Zinda—it means being alive…It must be true. You are alive.'

She smiled and whispered a prayer.

Slowly they pieced together torn bits of their lives,

sewing together jagged edges of pain. Each night after a hard day's work they would talk late, watching the hearth's glowing embers fade to grey ash, till sleep claimed them.

Sangay discovered new things about his homeland—the smell of fresh carpets of alpine flowers and blooming rhododendrons and the cold freshness of the mountain springs and the Drichu river.

They walked to their old home one day and stood by the knoll looking down at it. 'Homes have souls. Now that this is no longer ours, other souls have made it their own,' his mother said. The house was different from what he remembered—barer and more diminished in grandeur and aura. A high wire fence separated it from the open pasture. Chinese signage hung on a newly constructed gate that read 'Children's Home, Zinda.' Children played in the yard. Almost all of them were Tibetans.

'Orphans,' his mother said, 'Our house is a children's home run by the Chinese government now.' Sangay nodded, he was glad it was a home for children. Slowly they walked to their Ba and his silence prodded his mother to say, 'Don't feel too bad Sangay, sometimes we have to count our blessings. Thank god it's not a brothel.'

He knew the Chinese had slowly destroyed everything Tibetan, closing the monastery and ridding it of monks, making sure there was not a single picture of the Dalai Lama anywhere. The Chinese language was taught in schools, and there were many who were marrying Chinese since it was the best way to survive.

Slowly he learnt the ways of his mother, her life based completely on nature and her immense love for her animals. The more time he spent with her, the more he wanted her to come and live with them in India. When Tsungma joined them on a weekend with his wife and their infant son, they spoke about it. Tsungma was happy that his parents would be able to stay together. He promised to help with all the paperwork required. They agreed the best way to travel would be for Sangay to take her with him. She had never left Zinda before. But she would need permission to travel and that would take time. He had no way of contacting his father or Dikyi and letting them know his plans. He just hoped that all was well at home.

Sangay took his mother's photo with his small Yashica camera and had it printed. They applied for a passport. He was taken aback at his first meeting with a Chinese official. The officer began enticing him to come back home, promising a well-paying job. Sangay politely thanked him but said that his old father awaited his return. The official argued they could all stay together in Tibet, more well off than in India as refugees.

It was nearly a year before the Chinese gave her a passport and travel documents. She took one look at her photo and laughed, saying she looked like a scarecrow in a barley field.

The next step was to let go of her cattle. For too long they had been her anchor and she recognized each one of them from their mooing and bleats. Each one she gave away to relatives, leaving her despondent and teary-eyed. Everyone gave her a small sum as they said she would need some money when she left Tibet.

The last to go was her Ba with all her worldly

possessions. She gifted the tent to her newly-wed nephew and kissed his bride tenderly. 'When I married, I was a few years younger than you and Sangay's father was twenty. Now when I leave home, I am an old woman of forty-three.' The newly-weds hugged her, saying, 'You can never be old.' Sangay looked at his mother—the hardships she had borne had left their marks, her once fair yellow skin had wrinkled from years of hardship and the sun. Each wrinkle had a story to tell of pain, tears and loss. The starkness of her lined face only added to her unadorned beauty.

The whole family came to say their goodbyes. The women cooked and served tsampa, barley wine and a buffet of assorted yak and sheep meat. They sat around by a campfire remembering the old times when they were free and the homeland was theirs. For Sangay it was as if time stood still.

The next morning when he woke up his mother was missing. He found her sitting by the Drichu river, watching the sun come up. She said softly, 'I was just saying goodbye to everyone I let the river carry away.'

'Are you afraid?'

She shook her head and said, 'No...I am leaving here to finally go home to my family.'

Together they walked back to the Ba. His brother had bought her a small suitcase and packed her meagre belongings. She put in a round white pebble and a dried flower plucked from the meadow, 'For your father,' she said, as Sangay watched inquiringly.

She put a little earth in her coat pocket for luck. As

they crossed the Drichu river she cried and the tears fell till they reached Lhasa and took a flight to Kathmandu. When the plane circled Lhasa and she saw the Potala palace from the air she whispered, 'Om Manne Padme Hum' over and over again.

~

'Om Manne Padme Hum,' her lips moved in mumbled prayer constantly, like silent water over long immersed stones.

She reached for his hand and he smiled at her reassuringly. Flying had terrified her. When they landed in Delhi and she saw the traffic, she had asked wide-eyed, 'Where are all these people going?' He had laughed and said, 'Indians are busy people unlike the Tibetans.'

They had taken a taxi from the Delhi airport and it moved steadily past fields of sugarcane to finally climb a hill road and up the old tree-lined road to Rajpur. Through the rushing landscape, she caught her first view of the blue hills of Mussoorie. She knew they had arrived at their destination when she saw the prayer flags fluttering over roof tops and the colourful painted roof of the monastery.

Sangay patted her calloused hands, 'Aamo, we are here.' She nodded, smoothening her crumpled dark chuba.

It was a perfect April day, almost a year since he had left home. The taxi stopped by a small white home with a golden cloth fluttering at the doorway. He opened the gate, ushering her into the cemented courtyard. The click of the gate started a chain reaction. Dikyi rushed out, followed by excited cries of the children screaming, 'Apa, Apa!'

The door flew open and his father stood at the threshold. His eyes widened as he saw Sangay and took in his wife. He stumbled forward, his arms outstretched. She went to him and they stood there crying and calling to each other. It was the miracle she had prayed for through all the lonely years in Zinda.

His father put one arm around Sangay and another around his wife, beaming like a man who had got everything in his life. 'You got your mother back from Zinda, son. We are finally a family.'

Dikyi pointed to the plaque mounted on their gate. The brass plaque caught the sun and shone like burnished gold.

It read: 'Zinda.'

Sixty-Three

YEARS OF WAKING up at the same time had tuned his body clock. Even before Thupten looked at his watch, he knew it was three in the morning. For a while he lay in bed watching the butter lamp flickering by the altar, lighting up the Dalai Lama's benign face. He sighed, standing up and stretching. His friend Dorje was still asleep, his soft snore just a whoosh of air from an old tired man. Thupten reached down and pulled on his boots. Years ago he had discarded his slippers for boots because they gripped his feet better and kept his limp at bay.

He opened the door and stepped out. The cold Dehra mist had wrapped its white gossamer shroud over the dense sugarcane fields that surrounded their barracks. He took a deep breath and walked to the compound's hand pump, splashed cold water on his face and revelled in its sting. Then he reached for a small bowl, collected water for his altar and walked back. Once inside, he placed the fresh water at the altar with a mumbled prayer. He sat on a chair, wrapped a shawl around himself, closed his eyes and began telling his prayer beads. This had been his morning routine for years.

When he opened his eyes, he saw that Dorje was still

not up. He frowned. Dorje had taken to sleeping longer and becoming slower, but then he was already eighty-one. Years of punishing his body to its limit, flinging himself from 35,000 feet into a free fall, uncaring of how he met the ground—it was now taking a toll, like accumulated karma that caught up with you sooner or later. He walked up to his friend and watched Dorje's weather-beaten face, soft in repose. Sleep had smoothened his wrinkles and loose jowls. His head was covered in the regulation olive green woollen balaclava and his quilt was right up to his chin.

Dorje, just a year younger than him, had taken to lapsing into long silences. Sometimes he started speaking but got stuck midway, so others had to second guess and piece together what he said and what he left unsaid to understand what he meant. Thupten didn't mind; they were almost brothers and had known each other since they were five-year-old novices in the Gongkar Choede monastery in Lhokha. They had grown up so close that, like the marbles they kept in the pockets of their chubas, they ended up reflecting each other's colours.

Thupten could hear the pressure cooker whistle from the cookhouse. They were having dalia again for breakfast. He walked out, savouring the cold air; the mist was still thick but he could make out the oblong shapes of the other barracks, all grouped together in a large square with a park in between. The light of the cookhouse was a beacon in the sea of swirling mist. There were other figures gravitating towards the cookhouse. The cook was a genial man with a ready smile who had hot steaming cups of ginger tea ready for them.

'Tashi delek, Popo-la,' he said, as he brought him his tea in a white enamel mug.

Thupten smiled, called back a greeting, headed for the dining area and sat down, savouring the first sip of the hot, sweet tea. The newspaper was on the table and he reached for it, pulling on his glasses. Last night the television channels had talked of nothing but the surgical strikes India had conducted in Kashmir. He read the paper and marvelled at the precision strikes of the Indian army and how they had honed in on the launching pads of the terrorists and destroyed them. It was the first time that India had taken such a bold step. It was tough punitive action using resources that until now India had never openly acknowledged and showcased to the world.

It had started an animated debate, 'If India is capable of such strikes, why didn't they do it against China?'

'When?'

'When the Jamas overran Tibet and drove us out of our country.'

'1959? What was India's capability then? They took us in, that's what counted. Why would they have fought our war?'

'They could have done it in '62 when India and China fought a war.'

'But that was the war India lost. Since then, what is India's capability to take on China? What about its political will?' The men lapsed into silence as Thupten continued, 'Anyway, India has dealt with the numerous Chinese incursions into Indian territory by only posturing. Geographically, because of Tibet, the Jamas are in a superior position than Indians.'

Thupten looked around the room of animated faces suddenly silenced. They were old men and almost all of them cupped their ears to cut off the surround sound as a force of habit. They often laughed among themselves, making fun of each other. Over the years the hearty laughter of a hundred and twenty-six had dwindled to just sixty-three of them. One by one they had bid their friends goodbye. They were all well into their eighties and the only ones who had seen free Tibet. Now they had no country to go back to.

Just thinking of Tibet brought out such intense emotions and a deep yearning to return to that ancient land of sweeping plateau, snow-clad peaks and monasteries with gabled roofs humming with prayers. The land was magical, and nothing could replace the images of golden barley fields and endless meadows where the wind frolicked on wild whims, children raced each other on horseback and families picnicked together, their voices rising and falling in laughter.

Thupten would go for days without thinking of Tibet because that was the best way to live. To think about home was to weaken oneself, as then every waking and sleeping hour was filled with a yearning to return home, when there was no means to do so. In his mind he had written and rewritten hopes. If they were strung together as prayer flags, they would surely fill the sky. The sun had bleached them white and the wind had torn them to shreds. Yet they fluttered from time to time.

He looked out, his lips moving into a smile as he made out the dark shadow of his friend, Rinzing, bent against the cold wind as he did his kora around the monastery. They had constructed it with their own hands when they all came to live in the Herbertpur Old Age Home. The Home had been built for the retirees of the 22 Establishment, a hidden and secret force of Tibetans recruited back in November 1962 to train in mountain warfare against the Chinese. Immediately after India's defeat in October 1962's Sino-Indian war, the smarting Indian strategists had felt that they could tap into the simmering anger of the Tibetans and use their angst to hit the Chinese. Indians had systematically searched for young men who had some antecedents and history of fighting the Chinese, in order to open up another front and hit the enemy where it would hurt. By 1963, 22 Establishment was on its feet.

He himself had been recruited in 1963 from a road gang. In the border areas, road building was practically the only way to make a living. Large clusters of Tibetans were engaged in building roads. All day he and others like him crushed boulders into chips to be used on roads, or they uprooted trees that blocked paths. They constantly smelt of the black tar that had permeated their nails and skin, the pungent and repulsive smell clinging to them. The conditions were hard and people died like flies. Everything was alien, it was like stumbling into a strange new world, where everyone felt lost and hopeless.

The only way to survive was to take each day as it came and to labour so hard that you could not think of anything. The numb tiredness sent you into dreamless slumber. To think meant to relive the terrible sights of a burning homeland, of the dead scattered in a macabre bloody tableau: the exodus of people desperate to get away from the fury of the Red Army.

Most nights Thupten and his friends would huddle together in rags under plastic sheets and wait for dawn. When it rained they just sat under the plastic, letting the rain drench them, the cold from the wet soil seeping into their bodies and bringing on coughs and tuberculosis.

Life in Tibet had been so different. At the tender age of five he had been sent to a monastery. Slowly, along with other children his age, he had come to love the life there. Rising at four, he would sit with other novices on warm woollen carpets on the wooden floor of the monastery and recite the scriptures, learning them by rote. Every day as dawn came calling, theirs was the first land it would coax out from slumber. As the sun rose, the snowy peaks would take on the hues of gold and orange before the dappled sunlight entered their monastery, creeping slowly to overtake the butter lamps in their brilliance. It was a perfect life.

Thupten had decided he would study to become a doctor. He had begun to assist the monk who knew about medicinal herbs and its curing properties. Waiting on him, watching him heal the sick monks and poor peasants who flocked to him for solutions to their ills, gave Thupten satisfaction. On their visits to the upper reaches of Kham where the monks went to collect herbs, Thupten had been taught to recognize the medicinal plants which they sundried, powdered and mixed with other herbs or boiled for broth or kept soaked in oil.

It was while cleaning the monastery compound and

watering its gardens that he saw a convoy of trucks carrying Chinese soldiers, packed to the brim, travelling along the dirt tracks. The red flag with a yellow star fluttering in the afternoon breeze only made their guns with glinting bayonets more menacing. The dust that billowed in their wake created a storm.

Already there were fearful stories of them killing the local people in Kham and Amdo. The Chinese had been going around the two provinces rounding up men on suspicion of being members of the Tibetan resistance movement called the Chushi Gangdruk. The only resistance to the Chinese subjugation of Tibet came from these tall raw-boned men, the Khampas. Legend had it that, like all Tibetans, their forefathers traced their roots to the union that took place between a wise monkey and an ogress. The ogress gave birth to six children who were the first Tibetans, who gradually went on to populate the Tibetan plateau. Over a period of time as the Tibetans became Buddhists, the Chushi Gangdruk saw themselves as the Defenders of the Faith and the protector of the fourteenth Dalai Lama.

The Chinese became virulent in their effort to quell this army. Young able-bodied men were rounded up and carried away by the Red Army, never to return. The countryside was littered with men hung on stakes, flayed alive, dying with painful slowness, whispers of their deaths spreading like wildfire.

The more the Chinese quelled the Chushi Gangdruk resistance, the more it gained popular support. People visiting the Abbot in their monastery carried with them stories of the countryside, prompting him to ask them to be watchful of the Jamas.

The first time the Chinese came calling on the monastery, Thupten had been struck by how cold and menacing they looked. The Chinese officer stood ramrod straight, demanding a list of names and ages of all monks and warning them not to harbour, feed or assist any rebels from Chushi Gangdruk. That warning was a precursor to the things to come.

A night later the hills behind the monastery erupted with gunfire. Everyone scrambled out of their beds, rushing to the windows. The Abbot ordered them down on the floor lest they fell to stray bullets. The fierce gun battle raged into the night.

It was well past midnight when urgent pounding on the monastery doors prompted the Abbot to open them, only to confront wounded men of the Chushi Gangdruk asking for a doctor. The Chushi Gangdruk men were well-built and Thupten noticed that each man wore a charm box around his neck. Throughout the night he assisted the doctor monk in removing bullets and dressing wounds.

Two men died on the table from grievous wounds. The rest were stoic in their pain but too far gone to move out of the monastery unless they recuperated. The Abbot took the most difficult decision of swearing the monks into silence. They moved the rebels to the basement that served as their cellar. The two dead rebels were buried in the monastery garden.

Assisting the doctor monk, Thupten was impressed by the fortitude of the rebels. Two days later when the

Chinese came looking for them, Thupten and three other young monks led the wounded men through a secret passage to the woods beyond. Unwittingly crossing the threshold of their monastery, they became outlaws and part of the Chushi Gangdruk. There was no going back. By then the Chinese were everywhere and no story would corroborate their disappearance and sudden appearance.

At the camp, the monks met the leaders of Chushi Gangdruk. It was a world different to the quiet, peaceful life at the monastery. At seventeen, Thupten and his monk friends saw the men of Chushi Gangdruk as liberators and heroes. The first time Thupten stepped out of his monk's habit, wore layman's clothes and picked up the sword, he felt the excitement of being a warrior. It was also the day Gompu Tashi held out the protective charm box which encased the scroll of the 'White Umbrella' Goddess, blessed by the two holiest men in Tibet—the Dalai Lama and the Panchen Lama. They had joined the brotherhood of resistance fighters. Without a word, Thupten raised the charm box to his forehead and kissed it as Dorje knotted it behind his neck. He grinned and patted Dorje on his shoulder, tying his friend's charm in return.

The leaders inspired enormous awe. Among them were fighters. Just hearing that America was helping their cause left Thupten and Dorje awed and they hung on to Gompu Tashi's every command.

The warriors trained the boys in using swords and wielding them with lightning speed. Guns and ammunition were in short supply, to be used only in encounters with the Chinese.

Life wasn't easy in the cold arid desert. The nights were especially difficult as temperatures dropped. They lived in caves with fires going. The boys learnt to give sentry duties and look after the horses. Thupten and Dorje stuck together, as they had since they were five. They watched out for each other.

The first time they encountered the Chinese, they just followed the men in the lead as they launched themselves into battle, following instructions blindly as machine guns erupted around them. Hearts palpitating, they raced towards the bullets unleashed by the Chinese, swords in their hands and voices raised in war cry. Around them running men fell, their cries cut midway, but they raced on uncaring.

Like each man of Chushi Gangdruk, they too believed that the charms they wore around their necks, many of them encased in copper casings of bullets and beaten bombshells, would ensure they didn't die of Chinese bullets. The instructions were very clear: they had to strike and inflict whatever damage they could and fall back. They did not have the weaponry to engage with an enemy armed to its teeth for long.

Each contact was a dog fight as they ran towards the firing Chinese soldiers, assaulting them with their swords in close combat. When they regrouped, many would be missing. The injured never complained and those capable of still fighting continued to do so.

Chinese aggression had reached its peak and the Red Army killed without compunction. Fear of the Chinese had made villagers flee in search of protection. Hordes of women and children made a beeline for the Chushi Gangdruk camps. There they would spread out, pitching tents close by, cooking their meals while children played games nearby. The growing bulge of such followers became a death knell for the Chushi Gangdruk. Chinese patrol and air reconnaissance could easily spot such camps. They would come well-armed, and mercilessly gun down hapless women and children. Many men died protecting their families. Those who survived could easily pinpoint the massacre site due to circling vultures.

Survival lay in constantly moving camp. Each place they stayed for the night, they would hear terrible stories of Chinese torture and rumours that the Chinese were planning to abduct the Dalai Lama and take him to China. All around them a sense of uncertainty and fear prevailed. No one knew what was going to happen the next day.

A group of warriors that joined them as they moved towards Lhasa reported that thousands of people had camped around Norbulingka, the summer palace of the Dalai Lama, determined to protect the God King with their life. He had been invited by the Chinese to their camp for an entertainment programme, and had accepted the invitation. This had agitated the people who were sure that once he left Norbulingka he would be whisked away to China. They were determined to prevent him from leaving the palace.

The restless crowd got unruly, killing a high-ranking Tibetan official because of his leanings towards the Chinese. They had tasted blood.

At the Chushi Gangdruk camp a group of warriors left

silently, melting away into the night. Much later Thupten would learn that the group had gone to assist the Dalai Lama's escape to India.

In the early hours of the morning, firing started. Thousands of Tibetans who had camped outside the summer palace were butchered by the Chinese.

Chaos reigned in Lhasa. The Chinese army attacked the Chushi Gangdruk camp. Thupten and Dorje found themselves running into the fleeing multitudes in the streets of Lhasa. There was no time to think. The Red Army had surrounded them and a firefight had started, the bombs fell thick and fast and the smoke lowered visibility. The earth shook, sending out shreds, mud and splinters in all directions. Machine guns mounted atop trucks were firing in all directions—if the bombs did not get the escaping mob then the guns did, felling hundreds in the frenzied melee, their frightened screams drowned by bullets that rained all around like angry drones. Bodies piled up. Those who survived were targeted by lines of soldiers with bayonets as they moved forward, menacing and ruthless. With a fierce war cry a group of Chushi Gangdruk soldiers tried to break the cordon but were surrounded and outnumbered. At a given signal to withdraw, they fled in pairs, putting as much distance as they could between themselves and the slaughtering Red Army.

Thupten and Dorje crawled their way through a sea of dead. Blood from the dead drenched their clothes. A bottle of flaming petrol exploded a little distance away. People were hurling petrol bombs at the Chinese army and fighting with whatever they had. It was a war zone.

They rounded a street and saw a Chinese tank coming towards them; they ran to another street and saw it was already blocked with barbed wire. They turned into a narrow alley and ran smack into another crowd of desperate people.

Thupten and Dorje joined the human tide. Those who had horses rode carrying the old and the very young. Most just walked, carrying a few belongings, urging the elderly along. Fear was rife on their faces and many were openly weeping as black smoke rose in the sky, covering the morning with a pall of grey. The sound of machine guns and tank shells never stopped. The voices at the back urged the people in front to go faster as they walked out of Lhasa, taking to the mountain passes.

As far as the eye could see, the human exodus continued for miles. Soon the roadside was lined with families who were resting and conserving their energies. Thupten and Dorje walked on. They had with them the one sword that Thupten had carried. Dorje had lost his. They decided that it was pointless carrying it and left it by the mountain side.

On their fourth day of walking in the snow, they came across a frantic man whose wife was about to give birth. The man was stopping everyone for help. They shook their heads and moved on but Thupten could not get over the pain-laced eyes of the young woman about to give birth. For days after they had made it across into India, he wondered if the child had survived and if the family would be able to make it out alive.

On the fourteenth day they reached the Indian border—swollen waves of exhausted, famished and bewildered humanity. They were moved into a camp where it was incredibly hot and they were unable to eat the food the Indians dished out. Slowly it dawned on them there was no way back. As they stuck together and strangers became families, they were to bond for life in a new land where each needed a helping hand, a familiar word of greeting and a friendly touch to survive. From there they were sent to work in road gangs.

After that the road gangs were his life every day. How the days turned into months, and the months into years… they had stopped counting.

It was in the spring of the third year, just when the leaves reappeared on bare trees, that two leaders from Chushi Gangdruk came calling. With them were silent watchful Indian men. The leaders embraced them and asked if they would like to do something for their homeland. Both Thupten and Dorje had nodded eagerly. They were told to wait under the shade of a large tree. By evening Thupten saw their numbers swell to over five hundred as the leaders rounded up more men from surrounding Tibetan labour camps. Almost all of them had Chushi Gangdruk connections.

At dusk the men were herded into trucks and driven to an Indian army camp. The two friends wondered if they were being taken back to Tibet. When they were offloaded behind barbed wire premises, they spoke in excited whispers amongst themselves. They were served food and told to wait.

The sense of anticipation was palpable when the Chushi Gangdruk leaders appeared. Just their appearance created an uproar. The seniormost, Tashi, spoke up, 'You must be wondering why you are here. Let us not keep you in suspense any longer. We are here to recruit you to form a secret elite force that will be trained in guerrilla warfare to fight the Chinese.' A wild cheer went up. After all these years, there was hope.

Blind trust is a very Tibetan thing. If the leaders of Chushi Gangdruk had said they were going to their deaths, they would still have followed them with gusto. A day after the initial announcements the men were bundled into trucks and taken up to a mountain camp beyond Dehradun. The Chakrata camp comprised long barracks with tin roofs which were fenced with barbed wire. Dense coniferous forests lay below.

There were more surprises in store. They had never seen such a large congregation of Chushi Gangdruk men come together in India. Almost all of them were Khampas. When they got off the trucks, they were photographed for identification cards and issued uniforms and gear. Each man had his number sewn on his left chest pocket. An Indian officer, a thin dark man with agate coloured eyes, mentioned they would be called by the numbers they had been given. Their training began almost immediately.

Gradually the unknown bits fell into place as Thupten learnt that the Indians at the camp were from the Indian intelligence wing, and the American weapons instructors were the CIA. It was the first time many Tibetans had seen a white man up close. They were divided into classes of fifty. One of the first things the American weapons instructor did was to give them nicknames as he found their names too difficult to pronounce. Thupten was christened Jim while Dorje was Reeves. The Tibetans didn't mind the nicknames and numbers. For the first time they felt they had something to look forward to.

Their training wasn't easy. Up at four, they ran for miles in the mountainous terrain, followed by a tough exercise routine. Then there was a short break for them to grab their breakfast, wash up, and join the weapons classes once again. While the Americans taught them the handling of guns, detonation and information gathering, the Indians taught them free fall from planes and survival in high altitude terrain. It was a thrilling time for the Tibetans. Each new thing they learnt gave them a rush and made them feel they were closer to going back home.

As winter set in and snow blanketed the trees, turning the world white, they approached the end of their six months of rigorous training. They graduated using American weapons, having learnt to free fall in the dead of the night in high altitudes simulated to resemble the conditions in Tibet. With each paradrop they were tasked with reconnaissance and enemy contact. The Americans gave them maps and taught them to read, align and recognize features on the ground and engage with the enemy using surprise and ferocity. By then the Tibetans knew they had been raised to conduct covert operations behind Chinese lines in the event of another Sino-Indian war.

Soon there were changes. The American instructors left and the entire training was taken over by Indians. Thupten learnt the dark man with agate eyes was Captain

Nair. Their camp was the 22 Establishment. It was a name chosen by their Sikh Commander, Major General Sujjan Singh Uban, who had commanded the 22 Mountain Regiment during the Second World War and won the Military Cross. He chose for them the lucky number 22.

At the end of the first year, the 22 Establishment had some two thousand men trained in high altitude combat, already formed into battalions with companies. Each company was commanded by Tibetans and over them were officers from the Indian army on deputation to 22 Establishment. Each Tibetan felt they were ready to free fall into Tibet and rid their homeland of all the Jamas.

Every Tibetan in 22 Establishment had heard about the ongoing heroic struggle of some Chushi Gangdruk men who were still fighting for their homeland from camps set up in the remote reaches of Mustang in Nepal. From the windswept hills they crossed over treacherous passes to launch guerrilla attacks on Chinese posts in Tibet. Aided by the CIA in their quest for freedom, their survival was dependent on the local populace who still braved Chinese torture. It was in their homes and cattle sheds that the Chushi Gangdruk men hid if they could not fall back to Mustang. The more the SFF men heard of the Chushi Gangdruk's efforts the more they yearned to do their bit. They believed that, trained as they were, they could hit the Chinese hard and retreat to their base.

When nothing happened for almost a year other than carrying on battle preparedness training, some twenty odd men applied for casual leave. Under the leadership of their old Chushi Gangdruk leader they crossed over into

Chinese territory, raiding an unsuspecting Chinese army camp. The unexpectedness of the attack made the Chinese suffer casualties and the SFF men withdrew as silently as they had appeared, buoyant from their victory.

The reprisals were immediate. Overnight the SFF men were recalled, loaded into trucks, taken back to Chakrata and told very clearly that there was no way they could jeopardize India's fragile peace with China or expose the trained Tibetan fighting force to Chinese scrutiny. Crossing the international border and attacking Chinese posts could result in an all-out war between India and China. It was a war India could ill-afford.

The Tibetans understood they had to bide their time. They only hoped that, kept as furtive and secret as they were, they would still not be forgotten. They were a generation of recruits who chose not to marry. Their sole aim was to fight for their homeland. On occasions when their force commander visited them, they asked, 'Sahib, hum ko mauka kab milega?'—when will we get our chance?

The answer to their plea for an opportunity to prove themselves was always the same: 'Let's be patient.' When the 1965 Indo-Pakistan war took place they were considered too fledgling to engage. But by 1971, when another Indo-Pakistan war erupted, the SFF had over 10,000 trained men in six battalions who finally got their first action in war. Only that it was facing another front.

When Operation Eagle was launched, the hills of Chittagong teemed with 3000 SFF men. This operation was the pre-cursor to the 1971 Indo-Pakistan war for the

Chittagong Hill Tracts, and the SFF men were nicknamed the Phantom Raiders. The Tibetans scoured the hill tracts alongside the Mukti Bahini, the fighting force of the Bengalis, and infiltrated Pakistani dominated territories, destroying bridges, dams and communication lines. The fighting with Pakistani troops was intense as well as bloody. Within days of its engagement, SFF lost fifty-six men and had to contend with close to 200 wounded.

Thupten and Dorje were airlifted along with their comrades in helicopters and paradropped over a girls' college in Chittagong, where a company of the Pakistani army had entered and camped. News of rape and mayhem had rocked the city and reached the Mukti Bahini. Parachuting into the dark compound of the college before first light, the SFF surprised the Pakistani troops. They had not expected the enemy to rain down on them. The Pakistanis surrendered without even one shot being fired. For the young women, the SFF men were liberators and heroes.

A day later, General Niazi surrendered with 93,000 Pakistani troops, and the war was over. It was a historic win that created the new nation of Bangladesh. While the Indian troops were openly celebrating their win, the SFF quietly exited in troop carriers and were flown back to Chakrata.

Many of Thupten's friends died in that war; Sonam had his leg amputated. It was heartbreaking to see him hobble to the camp after his rehabilitation was over. He had become half a man. Worse, he could no longer free fall or carry out any duties. Men like him were honourably discharged with gratuity. It was sudden and final—in the prime of their lives they were without employment and had no pension to fall back upon.

The SFF was used again in Operation Blue Star, almost fourteen years later in 1984, to flush out terrorists from the inner sanctum of the Sikh holy shrine Harmandir Sahib. Both Dorje and Thupten had just five months left to retire but they volunteered for the Operation.

They crept into the temple complex through narrow alleyways—with no intel, the only way forward was blind. As the men went in, they were caught in a blaze of fire that came from unexpected quarters, from underground pits and fortified quarters overlooking the temple's main courtyard. The temple was a fortress. The army was caught in a crossfire, trapped and ambushed from all sides. But more troops rushed in, determined to fight to the finish.

As Thupten and Dorje crept forward to the main courtyard, dawn was just breaking, turning the dome of the temple into burnished gold. Surrounded by the shimmering moat, it stood out as an island of tranquility. For a moment peace prevailed before the firing began again. The men in their bulletproof jackets hit the ground, slithering under fire from everywhere. To their surprise, the sanctum sanctorum was heavily fortified.

Thupten was behind Dorje when he cried out in pain, clutching his leg. Even as he rushed to reach his friend, he realized the firing had come from the sewers beneath. Dorje was in acute pain, his breath harsh and jagged. Thupten covered Dorje, pulling him to safety. Dorje was swiftly evacuated and he was ordered to carry on.

Casualties mounted as the operation turned into a dog fight. The terrorists were well-entrenched in a strategic network of underground and overground fortified bunkers. It was a whole day later that they could finally flush out the terrorists.

In the hospital Dorje had lain in bed dazed from painkillers while doctors cut away muscles to remove the bullet that had shattered his tibia. A rod had been inserted in his leg and he had had to undergo rehabilitation for nearly a year to be able to walk around. He walked with the help of a cane and the winter days were especially painful, reducing his gait to a hobble. By the time he could stand on his feet, both Thupten and him were due to retire.

Retiring was a strange feeling, like coming down with a parachute which they knew would not open. They had no idea what they would do. Being recruited in the force had given them a reason to live. It had made them members of an elite tribe. Retiring meant the tribe was dumping them and moving on. They were detribalized.

They stood outside the gate of 22 Establishment, after twenty-two long years of service to the country they had embraced and called home. Everything they owned had been put in black tin trunks that had their names stenciled in white, along with a bedroll and a small bag. They had been given a gratuity of five lakh rupees with which they had to survive. There was no pension. The 22 Establishment was still a secret force. The Tibetans who served in it were a shadow force that could never be public.

Passing time was difficult. There was no timetable, nothing to rush to. The kora around the temple was their only exercise. Dorje did it with difficulty, leaning heavily on his cane. Thupten walked alongside, watchful and always helpful without trying to be. They would sit by the verandah at dusk and watch the birds come home to roost in the many trees they had grown together.

'When will we go to roost in the trees we have left behind?' Dorje had asked. Thupten had not said anything, so Dorje continued, 'I keep seeing the shaded leafy tree from which we would jump into the river.' Thupten smiled, he could feel the drench of the cold water and the peace as they floated on their backs, watching the cloudless deep blue skies, letting the river carry them downstream, till they were tired and swam across to the other shore.

Thupten looked at Dorje still smiling, 'For a silent guy you sure are very talkative today.' Dorje laughed, 'Just feel like talking today. When I am gone, you know there will be only sixty-two of you guys left.' Thupten frowned as Dorje kept speaking, 'A circle of life will come complete.' He was wrapped in his own thoughts.

Thupten was still frowning, 'What are you trying to say?'

Dorje grimaced putting out his hands. '1962 was the year our recruitment started, although we joined in early '63. Incidentally right now we are sixty-three inmates in this home. But with me gone, only sixty-two will be left—the year it all began for us all at the SFF.' Thupten opened his mouth to protest but Dorje held his hand up. 'When I am gone, I want you to have my prayer beads. My mother bought them for me. They are my only treasure.' Thupten had stayed quiet. Dorje talked a lot of dying these days.

Thupten stood up as people began walking in for breakfast. He had ruminated long enough. He was becoming an exact clone of Dorje, thinking of the past all the time. The clock said he had been sitting there for over an hour, his tea was long finished. He folded the newspaper and walked back to his room. Dorje was still in bed. He frowned. Something was wrong. Dorje looked as if he was sleeping but his right arm lay inert outside his quilt.

Even as he felt for a pulse, Thupten knew his friend was no more.

How long he sat there holding his friend's hand he did not know. The funeral that followed left him in a daze. As the flames went up, the tears fell inside, drenching him within. His only comrade was gone.

It was late evening when he walked back to the room. Someone had made up Dorje's bed, and instead of his sheets there was a blue bedcover. His walking stick rested against the bed. Thupten sat looking at the empty bed. There would be no more idle conversations between friends, no one to say 'Get up,' or 'Let's have tea,' or 'Let's go for a walk.' No one. No one till his own time came. He was sure Dorje would be waiting for him.

He looked up at the butter lamp still burning on Dorje's altar. He added some butter and prayed for his friend. Then he turned, his eyes sweeping the room.

Dorje's prayer beads in faded red silk lay nestled on his bedside table.

Jampaling

YANGKYI, EIGHTY-EIGHT YEARS old, held the phone to her ear: 'Amala,' a man said in Tibetan. She held the receiver closer, sure she had imagined it. 'Son?' she whispered. A broken anguished sob answered.

'I do not know who started crying first, I clung to the phone as if it was my child, but all that echoed back were broken sobs. I was hearing him after nearly fifty years of leaving Tibet. All we could do was cry for everything we had lost in our lifetime.'

Everyone has a story to tell. At Jampaling Elders Home in McLeod Ganj, Himachal Pradesh, India, where Yangkyi lives along with 153 other inmates close to the palace of their God King, the Dalai Lama, such happenings are nothing short of a miracle amidst others' stories that know only loss, pain, separation and emptiness.

Dressed in a grey chuba and beige blouse, Yangkyi still wears her hair in the traditional double braids. Her turquoise earrings are held up with red thread and her prayer beads never leave her hands. Yangkyi recalls how she and her peasant husband had gone to their local market at Pechang village, close to the town of Tsetang, Tibet, when chaos enveloped their lives and changed everything forever. 'When we reached the market, people were fleeing their homes, saying that the Chinese are here, the Dalai Lama has gone to India, if you stay here you will get killed. My husband insisted that we had to go immediately with the others. There was no way we could go to Thomu and get our thirteen-year-old daughter, or my mother. It was very far. Our fourteen-year-old son was also left behind as he was a monk in the Tashilumpo monastery.' Her voice rises and falls, and then there is a lull as her now failing vision focuses on the path they had taken a long time ago.

Following the mass exodus, Yangkyi and her husband trekked to India, helped by the Dalai Lama's protectors: the Chushi Gangdruk army that had set up camps on the way. For ten years Yangkyi and her husband worked at different road construction sites in India, till her husband's health began failing. 'He always said we'll go back together; we will find the children and be a family again. It wasn't to be... he died when I was sixty-nine.'

With no money and no one to look after her, her neighbours and friends got her to Jampaling Elders Home.

A few years ago an old friend went to Tibet to visit his family and came back with unexpected news for Yangkyi. Her son was alive, no longer a monk but a married man with three sons. He was the one to call her at Jampaling, opening the floodgates of tears that she had submerged years ago when she had buried all her hopes with her husband. Now he calls her at least two to three times in the year, especially during Losar, and reminds her of how she used to put new clothes under his and his sister's pillow, waking them up gently to tell them to wear their treasures. He tells her he can still remember the smell of those new clothes which she would buy and hide from them.

The last time Yangkyi spoke to her son she hesitantly asked about his sister and he assured her that she is married, has two children and is well but stays far away and so cannot talk to her. Yangkyi turns her prayer beads as she admits she is happy about her children, but as she does not want to probe too deep, she never asks what work her son does or how far his sister lives. She has heard that the old Tibetan culture has been replaced by the Chinese way of life. She admits she is fearful of asking too many questions as it could put her son at risk.

Almost always the talk ends with him begging her to come back to Tibet and live with them. He tells her he will come to get her, but she shakes her head, 'I can't see very well, I will be a burden on them, and besides my husband is buried here and His Holiness is here. It's the best place to die.'

Almost everyone who left their homeland was sure they would return, so they lived year after year hooked on to that hope. It was not to be. The first wave of those who fled Tibet, like Yangkyi, are now in their autumn ages and for them life has come a full circle. Their hopes are like the unanswered prayer flags which still flutter in the wind; waiting for their realization in stoic resignation. 'Even if I die here, I hope in the lifetime of His Holiness our people go back to Tibet,' says Yangkyi. As the only generation of people who saw free Tibet, the passing of Yangkyi and her friends will also mean that the old traditional ways of their ancient culture, carried with them, will be gone forever.

The second and third generations of Tibetans born in the sixties and after in India have never seen free Tibet, been privy to the unsurpassed grandeur of the raw Tibetan plateau, or lived the difficult yet simple lives of their parents. Their world in democratic India is shaped by what they see around them. More educated than their parents, they are like all young people of their generation, technically savvy, forward-looking, well-versed with the Tibetan ways of life, but less inclined to be romantic or sentimental about their past. The tiny threads that weave the whole composite culture will be severed once the old generation passes on.

There are many like Yangkyi—old, frail and alone. Most of the inmates of Jampaling are men in their late seventies and eighties, since more men than women fled Tibet in the exodus of 1959. They speak of their lives as if they unfolded only yesterday, their memories sharpest and most colourful of the days they left back home.

Tsepak from Sarzo village of Amdo's Sichuan province is an octogenarian. When he smiles, his eyes crinkle in the corner and transform him briefly into the youthful charmer he must have once been. He had left his village and set up a small shop in Lhasa selling tea leaves and clothes. In 1959, aged thirty, he and his fiercely independent girlfriend, Kelsang, pregnant with his child, were looking forward to raising a family. Overnight their lives changed when the Chinese began closing flanks into Lhasa. On order by the Tibetan government, Tsepak joined the army as a guard to protect Norbulingka, the Dalai Lama's summer palace, from the Chinese Liberation Army.

Recalling the incident, Tsepak makes a circle with his hands. 'We surrounded Norbulingka determined to protect our Dalai Lama. We were not the only ones—there were monks, nuns, men, women and children. Some of us knew that the Dalai Lama had already left the palace but we continued to surround it like a protective shield so that the Chinese did not know of his escape. The Chinese bombed and attacked Norbulingka fiercely. There were many people who were killed, and later the Chinese came and searched the dead. We knew they were looking for the body of the Dalai Lama.'

Tsepak escaped in the ensuing chaos with a friend, putting as much distance between them and the marauding Chinese army as possible in a bid to reach Lhokha. 'The exodus was like a torrential river. It swept up all of us like hapless debris. Everyone was heading towards India where His Holiness had gone. I wanted to go back to Lhasa to get Kelsang but it was impossible. I told a monk to tell her to keep everything she could salvage from the shop. People who joined us in the long trek to India mentioned that the Chinese were sending people from different areas back to their villages so I was relieved that Kelsang had perhaps gone back to Amdo.'

For fifteen days and nights Tsepak and his group of nine friends walked relentlessly. Braving fatigue, hunger and the constant fear of being pursued by the Chinese, they reached India. While his friends worked at road construction sites in the picturesque hill town of Kalimpong in West Bengal, Tsepak eventually started a small roadside restaurant selling Tibetan food. 'We got a salary which was barely enough. It was back-breaking work as there were no roads, we had to blast mountains to create them. We lived in tiny shacks and worked long hours. The smell of tar never left our bodies. The only thing that kept us going was that we constantly talked about what we left behind, sure that if not this day or the next day, then by next summer we would return home. Many summers went by and nothing happened... and now sixty years have passed.'

Unable to get good dividends, Tsepak abandoned his restaurant and joined the Indian paramilitary force when he heard they were recruiting Tibetans. He was enrolled in 22 Establishment that was headquartered in the hill regions of Garhwal as a cook. After twenty years of meritorious service Tsepak finally retired in 1983. He never married because he believed he would go back, hoping that his Kelsang was waiting for him with their child. He hoped it was a daughter. She would surely be a young woman now who knew of him.

It was after his retirement that Tsepak heard Tibetans could visit their homeland. He made a trip to Tibet with the one quest of finding Kelsang. 'The streets of Lhasa were unrecognizable. I found Kelsang—she had never married but had two children, a son and a daughter, both of whom worked in a karaoke bar. Our own daughter had died of illness when she was six years old.' Kelsang wanted to come back and live with him in India but the official documents were difficult to make. He returned back to McLeod Ganj, sure he had done the best thing as he had nothing to offer Kelsang.

Thereafter Tsepak never attempted to call her like she had asked him to. Unexpectedly, an old friend ambled into Jampaling to tell him that Kelsang had called him and begged him to ask Tsepak to speak to her. When the call went through, she just kept calling his name and crying. 'For a long while I heard her crying and then I put the phone down as I couldn't bear it any longer. I never called her again. I can offer her nothing and I am afraid if I call her often she may get into trouble with the authorities.' He remains silent for a long while as he turns the small prayer wheel again and again, his lips moving in prayer.

Tsepak shares his tiny cell-like room with another Jampaling companion he met once he came to this home. There are thirteen such elders' homes across fourteen Tibetan establishments in India; this one is considered the most fortunate place to die as it's close to their God King. Almost all the inmates of Jampaling have tiny altars in their room with a photograph of the Dalai Lama decorated with a khada or the traditional scarf. The room contains everything they own, a few souvenirs that stand like individual milestones with innate memories that neither time nor age can dispel, made more poignant by old sepia-tone photos of families nailed to the wall. With no heating and no attached toilets, the Home is dependent on funding from sponsors and is strictly budgeted to last the whole year. Even its inmates are those whose solitary lives were steeped below the poverty line.

Beyond the room up a flight of steps is the community prayer hall. The sunlit glass windows open up to the valley below. Photos of the Dalai Lama, right from his youth to present times, are festooned with gold, red and blue cloth; the colours of the Tibetan flag dot the room. Comfortable cushions and shawls mark individual places. Low tables contain their scriptures, prayer wheels and tiny lantern lamps that move in the ancient rhythm of their mumbled prayers.

A typical day starts with a prayer at 7 a.m. in the mist-laden mountain settlement which lasts for an hour and a half, followed by tea and breakfast by nine. After which it is 'doctor time,' and the elders have a choice between a Tibetan doctor or a western practitioner. Others put on their walking shoes to do the kora or the traditional circumambulation in a clockwise direction around the main temple and the palace of the Dalai Lama. The kora takes approximately an hour as the road rises and dips, ambling past serene mountain sides strung with fluttering prayer flags and flat round stones inscribed with 'Aum Manne Padme Hum,' the most fervent prayer of all Tibetans. People dedicate these stones once their wishes come true or when they aspire for something.

The kora is followed by lunch at the community kitchen, with inmates helping out in cooking. Most take their lunch outside and sit in the sun and eat as if they were on a picnic. This is followed by game of cards, carrom or just rest. Prayer time brings them all together at 2.30 till 4 followed by tea and dinner by 5.30 p.m. It is a spartan life, since most are content to just immerse themselves in prayers and are given to long silences in an age-old understanding that their days are passing them by.

Except for Tsering Tsomo, who goes nowhere without

her long-handled broom. Her hair wrapped in a colourful bandana, Tsering sweeps the entire kora every day. She grins and in between swift strokes of the broom she says, 'When I came to Jampaling I saw that old people argue a lot, so I had two choices—sleep, or just get up and clean. I decided to clean.' Tsering thinks she is sixty-four but looks years older. Her old faded identity card photocopy shows off a pretty woman, with long waist-length hair tied back in two folded plaits.

Age has changed her once soft skin to weather-beaten creases but cannot touch her spirit. Her knuckles are gnarled and knotted from years of washing clothes for the local Tibetan establishment in Kalimpong, West Bengal. Her hands remain raw and pink from the cold winds of McLeod Ganj which is 8000 feet above sea level. However, this does not deter her from cleaning the kora, in any weather: 'When it's very cold and misty, especially during the winters, I finish sweeping by 10 in the night, by which time I have finished saying all my prayers. I sweep because I want to give something back to my community, and except for labour I have nothing to give. Some years from now I will be dead but I hope His Holiness and all my people go back to our homeland.'

In 2019, it will be exactly sixty years since the Chinese occupation forced the fourteenth Dalai Lama to flee his homeland and take refuge in India, resulting in a mass exodus of 80,000 Tibetans like Yangkyi and Tsepak.

For every Tibetan who left his homeland, the transition from being a free nomadic and agrarian life in the windswept plains, protected by snow-peaked mountains,

Jampaling

gushing swift rivers and streams, to becoming a displaced population in an alien country, was not easy.

Till the Tibetans were expelled from their homeland, a majority of them had lived in isolation, secluded from major social and political events around the world. The Second World War had passed Tibet by, a society that was still steeped in its ancient Buddhist ways, with the only window to the world being trade.

Their faith however, kept them alive. The Tibetans who initially came into exile gradually spread to fourteen settlements scattered all over India, in the states of Jammu and Kashmir, Himachal Pradesh, Sikkim, West Bengal, Maharashtra, Karnataka and Meghalaya. Today, official figures according to the Planning Commission of the Tibetan Government in Exile, puts the number of Tibetans living in India at 100,000. Roughly 50,000 Tibetans are scattered all over the world in Nepal, Bhutan, Switzerland, North America and the European countries. What they have been able to do is create thousands of Tibetan religious centres for meditation, religious purposes and even research.

In the narrow lanes of McLeod Ganj, tiny shops sell knitted sweaters, socks, hats, heavy padded jackets with faux fur, jeans, and even duplicates of Puma, Nike and Reebok shoes: all ironically from China. Eating joints cater to foreign palates with Italian pizzas and pastas, cakes, pastries and chocolates on offer. All roads lead to the main temple and the palace where the Dalai Lama resides. It is on these hallowed grounds that the Dalai Lama imparts his teachings, while in McLeod Ganj he still meets people who made the difficult trek, braving being shot, maimed or killed by Chinese soldiers. The official figures are that each year almost 2000 men, women and children bet their lives to make their quest with destiny. Those who make it to McLeod Ganj usually never return to their homeland. Their numbers have been dwindling in recent times.

Kathup Tsering, twenty-four, from Maypo village in Zorgyi area of Amdo, is one such example. His peasant father sent him with his uncle when he was nine to study in Tsoe city in Gannan Autonomous Prefecture. Kathup went on to study at yet another Chinese graduate school at Wuhan city, which is the capital of Hubie province. Kathup spoke fluent Chinese and had only Chinese friends. His long-distance relationship with his family was never sustained and he never knew his roots, save for the fact he was not Chinese but Tibetan. Determined not to go to a Chinese university, Kathup left his school with the 5000 yuan he had saved over years and took a bus to Lhasa.

'It took me five days of changing many buses to reach Lhasa. My father's friends used to do business there and I was determined not to get caught by them, so after five days I left for Shigatse. I met a man a little older than me, also from Amdo. We became friends and he told me he was preparing to go to India. He had no plans...just walking to India. I had nothing to keep me home. For three months we prepared for our trek. We were afraid to share our plan with anyone. Every day we would buy something for the trek. We bought tsampa, butter, two blankets, sugar, cheese and even dry tinned food that is used by Chinese army, heavy boots and jackets. One night in June 2001, we picked up our bags and followed the main road to Lhatse.

'We stayed the night in a hotel in Lhatse and before dawn we took the forest route up a mountain path. We were not scared. We passed some people like us but we did not stop. A shepherd pointed out the way to India when we asked; he was not at all surprised. We did not know where the Chinese guards were. We rested during the day and walked at night, using torchlight only when it was absolutely necessary. When we reached Nanglapa, the mountain between Nepal and Tibet, we knew we had to be careful. It was here that most people suffered from frostbite. In the year 2006 the Chinese army killed a nun and a man who were crossing over. We joined a group of Tibetans like us and reached Nepal. It was around the time that the King of Nepal had been assassinated so there was a lot of turmoil. However, after one week we were taken by bus to Delhi and from there to McLeod Ganj. One week later we had an audience with the Dalai Lama and since then I am learning what it means to be Tibetan. For me there is no going back, my roots are here. They were uprooted from Tibet when people had to leave.'

Kathup's friend Thupten owns a café in McLeod. He was born in 1965 when his parents worked in a small settlement in Kalimpong making roads. He was one of the few children born to the Tibetan community which was still in the state of rehabilitation in India. His wife Tsering and he have two children. Born in exile, Thupten admits what he knows of Tibet is what he has heard from his eighty-nine-year-old father. 'When my father dies all the stories that he told us about our family die with him. Of course we will always know of it, but how much of it will our children know?' He admits, like his teenage daughter Dolma, that there is a difference between the Tibetans who came from Tibet and those who were born here. 'We were born in independent India and it is bound to influence the way we see the world. For us freedom means our birthright. The way India got its independence from British rule means it is possible for us too. Only a vast majority of us do not live in our homeland, but the desire to return home and be free is universal for all Tibetans.'

Tsering agrees that worldwide protests were spontaneous and resulted from years of keeping a tight leash over their patience. 'We are three generations of Tibetans clamouring for one thing—our right to return to our homeland. In 1961, I was four when my mother walked carrying my infant brother and me for two months, hiding in forests and walking blind at night to reach India. My brother couldn't survive the ordeal, he died when we reached India. My generation has seen the hardships our parents endured. The second generation born in India have also been through a struggle, as the community was finding its feet. The third generation knows of their identity and responsibilities. We all want one thing…to go back to our homeland. We have our differences; some want complete freedom. His Holiness has advocated the middle path, autonomy of Tibet under the People's Republic of China. Whatever our differences, they are all part of a democratic process and our goal is freedom.'

Jampaling

On his part the Dalai Lama has called, 'The worldwide agitation as a manifestation of deep-rooted resentment of the Tibetan people under the Chinese government...' He called the happenings in his homeland a 'cultural genocide.' Years ago the Dalai Lama had said that Tibet's 2,100-year-old culture was dying within Tibet. Weighed by the collective aspirations of his people, the Dalai Lama has been working tirelessly to negotiate with the Chinese government for their return to their homeland. He has appealed to the UN to intervene. Sixty years, he admits, is heavy to bear since it is a lifetime of living on hope.

In his sedate home in the hills that offers a magnificent view of the Dhaulagiri range, I meet the Kalon Tripa, the former Prime Minister of Tibetan Government in Exile. A large portrait of the Dalai Lama frames the room. In his maroon robes, Professor Samdong Rinpoche sits comfortably and chooses his words with care. 'The entire demography of big states like Lhasa, Shigatse, Chamdo are non-Tibetans. The recent statistics of Lhasa town, the capital of Tibet Autonomous Region, has 81 per cent of its population as non-Tibetans—largely Hun Chinese and other minorities, and only 19 per cent of people are Tibetans. Under such circumstances, Tibetan people cannot survive without knowing the Chinese language. It is taught in all the schools, but there is no arrangement to teach Tibetan language or culture. Growth, lifestyle and the way of thinking—everything has changed due to the overwhelming culture of the majority of non-Tibetans. Tibetans living in the countryside have no access to education or access to monastic life. Everything is controlled and they are still living in poverty. In the streets of Lhasa the majority of beggars belong to the Tibetan ethnic group. Inside Tibet, the Tibetan culture is almost dying or is dead.'

The Professor admits that culture largely depends on people and people depend on their homeland, as each nation needs to have geographical territory. Without territory, living as diaspora or under a repressive master makes it difficult to preserve and pass along culture to the coming generations. 'Sixty years is more than half a lifetime. These sixty years have been the most critical and troublesome as people have passed through a great deal of misery, pain, torture... and a great number of people have perished. Since 2008, more than 150 people have burned themselves alive protesting for Tibet's freedom. Even as they protest and ask for their rights, they burn themselves instead of harming anyone, offering their bodies as a flame for the darkness that surrounds Tibetans.

'We have to be thankful to PRC who have exposed us to the world at last. In spite of the tragedy, the Tibetan refugees have established religious, cultural and educational and research centres. Tibetans born after 1959 are 100 per cent literate. All over the world there are more than a thousand Tibetan religious centres, study and research centres, and we have a number of support groups for the Tibetan cause. His Holiness, a Peace Laureate, is leading the world towards peace, compassion and non-violence. All these are miracles which could not have happened in the 3000-year history of Tibet, but have happened in these sixty years.' For a while the articulate monk is quiet and his eyes are like a deep still pond as he says slowly, 'I was twenty when I left Tibet. I remember everything. I may forget the room I lived in, at the hotel I stayed in yesterday, but I remember every tree in Tibet—their shape, each stone on the floor, each pillar, their colour, and the size of my monastery very clearly in my mind.'

As the world takes sides and Chinese authorities try and salvage their public image, Tibetans believe that their cause may have got a platform for the first time in sixty years of exile. In Jampaling, the elders have heard of the agitation, self-immolation and talks—some wish they were younger and could be a part of it, others wait in expectant silence.

Yangkyi calls herself and the others at Jampaling the seeds which the wind scattered far away from the native tree. While they have taken root in a distant land, they have blossomed although they never shared the same sky or quenched their thirst from the swift mountain springs. 'I always remember my house with its door wide open, surrounded by maize and millet fields dancing in the breeze. Always when I am walking towards it, I can hear my children's happy voices as they sang,

> *Although her body is adorned by red and yellow corals*
> *our mother is our priceless treasure.*
> *In the hard rock with sparkling diamond dew,*
> *the vulture makes it nest.*
> *The father vulture takes care of all obstacles*
> *so baby vultures can be*
> *the happiest little birds in the world...'*

Yangkyi voice rises and falls and trails into a whisper. With her passing, such songs will indeed be like the seeds that the wind scattered far away from their native land.

WHITE
Air

The Social Entrepreneur

Lobsang Wangyal sat in the taxi as it sped towards the Indira Gandhi International Airport, and for the first time he was free of the apprehension travel usually brought.

At the crowded arrivals area Lobsang paid the driver, pulled out his suitcase, heaved his compact haversack on his back and walked in. At forty-seven, he was a tall, dapper man, whose dashing style made him easy on the eye. Clad in jeans, a soft denim shirt and boots, with his travel pouch clipped to his belt, he carried his folded jacket slung casually over the handle of his suitcase. His shoulder-length hair was tied back in a pony tail. Almost twenty years ago he had pierced his right ear, and still sported the diamond he had bought from his first pay as a stringer photographer with Agence France-Presse.

He showed his ticket to the gun-toting security man and headed for the ticket counter of Continental Airways. He unzipped his pouch and pulled out his passport. How many times had he held that precious document, smelling it, letting his finger run over its blue cover to trace the Ashoka lions...?

He held it out at the immigration counter and held his breath. It was his passport's first litmus test.

The man at the counter held up the passport and smiled, 'Chandragiri, Orissa, I was born there too. My home town.'

Lobsang smiled, 'Mine too. Tibetan settlement there.' The man was in the process of stamping the passport. He paused, turned the passport around and looked at Lobsang. He had taken him for a North Easterner. Migration was slowly changing the demography of small towns and he had stopped being surprised anymore. But a Tibetan with an Indian passport, now that was a first. He flipped the page—the passport was just two months old. He looked at Lobsang and saw his eyes watching him steadfastly, as if daring him to reject it.

'I thought Tibetans use the yellow-coloured Identity Cards when they travel.'

Lobsang nodded, 'Yeah, so did I till I got my Indian passport.' The man looked closer and smiled—oh yes, he had read about the man opposite him in the newspaper alright.

'So I get the privilege to put the first stamp in your passport,' he said. Lobsang smiled back.

'Have a good trip, sir,' the man said, stamping the passport and slipping it across the counter.

'Thank you,' Lobsang said, and held out his hand. The man shook it.

Lobsang went through security and headed for a coffee shop. He sat down with a sense of relief. The passport had worked. It validated everything he had struggled for.

He had a lot of time to kill. He pulled out his laptop and logged on to his email. He scrolled down, quickly reading a mail from his new partners who were welcoming him to New York. He grinned as he saw Tenzin's email. It was an animated e-card—a lone shadow of a man with long hair in a bobbing dingy defying a stormy sea accompanied with blinding rain, thunder and lightning, to finally reach calmer waters and the rainbow in the sky. It contained just one line: 'Bon Voyage.'

He smiled, closing his laptop. Trust Tenzin to be dramatic.

Taking a sip of his coffee, Lobsang recalled how he had spent the summer of 2016 in his cousin Tenzin's small one-bedroom flat in New Delhi's crowded Tibetan quarter Majnu ka Tila. For a fortnight he had maintained a punishing schedule, buoyed by his righteous search for a lawyer who would take up pro bono the case of a Tibetan applying for an Indian passport.

Tenzin's spirits were flagging when finally through his contacts he learned about Giriraj Subramanium, who did complicated cases pro bono. Both young men were apprehensive and unsure if their request would be entertained. They waited in the lawyer's crowded office space, inundated with men carrying files in black coats who went in and out looking officious. They were told it was Subramanium's day in court so he was too busy to meet them. They had seen him briefly as he had left and returned in a flurry of activity, a man with rimless glasses and a confident stride. He had rushed in, speaking fast as a train of people nodded at his instructions. He had turned his head and frowned as he saw Lobsang and Tenzin, said something to a calm middle-aged woman and disappeared into his office.

The woman had done everything in her power to make them leave but Lobsang felt this was his only hope. So he refused Tenzin's suggestion that they come back the next day. They sat there the whole day with just a cup of coffee between them. Around eight at night when Subramanium was leaving Lobsang stood up. 'Sir, I want to request you to take my case. I am a Tibetan born in 1970 in Chandragiri, Orissa. I want an Indian passport,' he said.

Subramanium arched an eyebrow, paused and turned back to his office. The lady was in the process of turning off the lights.

'Okay, tell me what is it that you are looking for?'

Lobsang explained, 'India's citizenship law says that anybody born on or after 26 January 1950 and prior to 01 July 1987 here is a citizen of India. As a Tibetan, I was born in India in Orissa in 1970 and would like to apply for an Indian passport.'

Subramanium nodded, waiting for Lobsang to continue. 'Currently, all Tibetans are issued a stay permit called Registration Certificate which has to be renewed every five years.' He pulled his out from his wallet and put it on the table. Subramanium flipped it open and asked, 'Is this used when you travel out, like a passport?'

'No, when we travel abroad the Indian government issues to us an Identity Certificate which is also called the Yellow Book, in place of the passport.' He took one from his wallet and held it out. 'This takes at least a year to get, and each time you travel, you have to run around and ensure you get an exit visa and a return visa. Each time we travel, us ordinary people, it's a nightmare with so many people to please.' He paused, 'You understand what I mean,' Subramanium let a ghost of a smile light up his eyes in acknowledgment, letting Lobsang steam on, 'I am just tired of running around in circles.'

Subramanium flipped the intercom and asked the lady to bring in three green teas. The tea warmed them after hours of waiting in the air-conditioned hall.

'Sir, I have little money, so won't be able to pay your fee. Will you take my case?'

'How long have you been trying for a passport?'

'Nearly a year and half, and all I do is go around in circles. None of the online forms are for us. The passport office says the Ministry of External Affairs will take out a policy for issuing us passports but that has never happened. We have a court order that says that we Tibetans can vote. It's okay to vote but not okay to get a passport. Is that justice?'

'So you want me to do a suo moto?'

Lobsang nodded and waited. He had read the Indian Citizenship Act threadbare and knew he was right.

Subramanium looked at Lobsang without saying a word and read his scars—the years of deprivation, of sitting on the margins, the geography of loss and the history of hurt that clung to him despite his dapper disguise.

'How far do you want to go?'

Lobsang frowned, 'Far?'

'Yes, how much further will you be willing to go on this case?'

'All the way and further if need be.'

Subramanium had his answer, 'I will do it,' he said as

he held out his hand. Lobsang held his breath as he asked, 'Do you need anything else, anything from me?'

'No. Just stay focused. I will do the rest and don't ignore my hand.' Lobsang grinned, reaching out and clasping Subramanium's hand.

It was almost a month later that Subramanium filed the suo moto petition. Lobsang met him for coffee in his chamber. It was a more relaxed meeting. Subramanium looked at Lobsang carefully. 'Tell me Lobsang, I know so little about you, tell me about your family, your life.'

Lobsang smiled, 'Nothing much to tell. I was born in Chandragiri, Orissa. My parents met and married in 1969 in Dharamshala. They were fresh from school, my mom from Kalimpong and my father from Darjeeling. After they married, they applied for jobs with the Central Tibetan Administration. My father was sent as Tendhar or the English Secretary to the Tibetan establishment in Orissa. My mother became a community health worker. I was born a year later. When they had their third child, my parents asked the Tibetan administration for help. That was when I, aged seven, was bundled off to Mussoorie to study.'

'How was it?'

'Terrible. I was perpetually cold, hungry, bullied. Every Sunday we would get one boiled egg and a banana—that was the treat I waited for. After we got US Aid, the food improved. I failed twice, so I was in school for fourteen years. Then I studied in a college in Shimla.'

'Where did you go after college?'

'McLeod Ganj.' The epicentre for all Tibetans, a town

of both hope and despair. A town of their pride, temple, trinkets, tourists, cafes, hotels and prayer flags. A small hill town with just a few roads, a place where every local knew each other. Here the smallest whisper was a murmur.

'What work did you take up?'

Lobsang shrugged, 'I was very interested in photography. My father gave me the money to buy my first camera, an Olympus OM 1, 100 per cent manual, great camera. I mastered it and applied to the Central Tibetan Administration for a job as a photojournalist. I got no reply for over a month. It was frustrating. We are roughly one lakh Tibetans in India and jobs are so scarce. I guess you can't blame the government as they can only find jobs for a few. The rest have to manage. Those who get jobs never leave as it is secure employment. In retrospect I can see that but I was so mad at the lack of response that I wrote an angry letter and gave it to *Mang Tso*, a fortnightly newspaper. They published it and the letter became a hit. I began working for them.

'I worked with them for a year and then tried my hand with the radio but felt I had to do something different, more satisfying. In 2000, I decided that with my love for art and culture I would create a platform for change, a new Tibet that was not shackled to its past. That's how I became a social entrepreneur.'

Subramanium looked at Lobsang for a long time; he knew there was much left unsaid so just said, 'I like the phrase 'social entrepreneur.'

Lobsang smiled, 'So do I. It's better than 'dreamer.'

It was almost seven months later that Subramanium

called him up in McLeod to tell him that the Supreme Court had directed the Regional Passport Office to issue his passport post-haste.

Lobsang thanked him profusely, Subramanium cut him off with, 'Say thank you after you get your passport in your hand.'

It was a precursor of things to come. The police report categorically stated that Lobsang Wangyal lived in a rented flat, had no permanent residence and hence could not be verified.

Disheartened, he called up Subramanium, 'Sonia Gandhi, an Italian, gets a passport when she marries an Indian, and I who was born in India get rejected for not owning property. I want us to go a step further and fight it out and at least die trying.'

Subramanium didn't falter—he filed a contempt petition in the court and eventually Lobsang was issued with a passport by a shaken Regional Passport Office, Shimla.

The day he got his passport by mail, he took the night bus to Delhi to personally meet Subramanium. 'I can't thank you enough,' Lobsang said, carrying a small thanka of Goddess Tara for the lawyer who had become a friend.

Subramanium's austere face spread into a smile as he held his hand out, but Lobsang stepped forward and hugged him.

He was finally an Indian.

He had lived in India all his life and this passport gave him an Indian identity. He did, however, hang on to his Green Book, determined to pay his taxes as a Tibetan to the Central Tibetan Administration—those were his roots.

~

Comfortably ensconced in his seat as the Continental Airways plane took off, Lobsang found himself next to a middle-aged Indian couple who lived in New York and were returning after a trip to their home in Gandhinagar, Gujarat. The man introduced himself as Anand Modi, and his languid wife, who had her nose buried in a book, as Mohini.

'Lobsang,' he said and held out his hand, after the man had introduced himself.

'Which place in the North East are you from?'

'I am Tibetan.' Lobsang said smiling politely.

'Oh. And where do you live?' The surprise was evident.

Lobsang grimaced inwardly. Anand, like all Indians, was inquisitive.

'Dharamshala.'

'Oh yes, it's where the Dalai Lama lives, no?' He didn't wait for confirmation, continuing,

'I really look up to him and his teachings. Not that I know too much about Buddhism but I believe in its core values. I think it is not just a mindful religion, but its logic makes it easy to follow.'

Lobsang nodded. For the ninth time he wished he had brought a book too. He picked up the inflight magazine but his neighbour was a talkative man.

'So what do you do, Lobsang?'

'I'm a social entrepreneur.'

'What's that?' It was Mohini who had spoken this time as she looked at him with interest.

'Well, I have great love for art and culture, so in the year 2000 in Dharamshala I started a Free Spirit Festival since I wanted to see a New Tibet, not one shackled by our past. I brought modern musicians and singers to the town that year. The next year as it grew, I brought artists from Delhi and Bangalore.'

'So, a music festival.'

'Initially yes, but I also bring in people, important people from the Tibetan community, to showcase our culture. One year, I brought Tashi Tshering, a Lama Mani. Do you know who they are?'

Both his companions shook their heads, 'Well, they are traditional Tibetan storytellers. The tradition was started way back in the twelfth century by a great learned Lama Richen Tsangpo. In the olden days they would travel from village to village carrying small shrines and thankas or painted scrolls and tell stories based on the ethical code of conduct or the moral concept of karma and compassion for all living beings. When the Tibetans fled their homeland, there were only nine known Lama Manis who came to India. Tashi Tshering was the last one. He died in 2001. It was the end of an era.'

'Wow, but I am sure the Tibetan community must have done a lot to preserve their culture.'

'Yes, a lot has been done by the community. But when people like Lama Mani die then a part of everything they know, however well-documented, dies with them.'

'Do you still do your Free Spirit Festival?'

'No. After the 2001 event I thought of how to take it forward and I realized that until now there was very little involvement of Tibetan women in public spaces. In 2002, I decided that I would start the Miss Tibet contest.'

'And did you?' Lobsang nodded, watching Modi's incredulous expression of disbelief change to astonishment. 'Wow. That's a very bold move in a conservative Tibetan society.'

Lobsang laughed, remembering how ballistic the Tibetan Government in Exile had been, and how much they had opposed it.

There was a lull in conversation as refreshments were served. So Lobsang didn't tell them that as a Tibetan in India there was nowhere to gravitate save for McLeod Ganj. His initial announcement of the Miss Tibet contest styled on international lines was seen as aping the west and destroying Tibetan culture. The biggest outrage being that it was a contest of showing flesh when Buddhism preached inner beauty. The scattered refugee community's greatest fear is that by aping the West they could lose their own religion and identity.

Even the Chinese protested against the use of the title, insisting that Tibet was theirs. But Lobsang stuck it out. There was a righteousness in his stance. A determination to follow his gut instinct as he refused to give in to intense social pressure. He braved the name-calling, insisting, 'It was time we changed and moved on, we needed to celebrate diversity. The pageant would showcase Tibetans as people who were not just struggling and who could create a place in the world. The Miss Tibet platform was that international platform where Tibetan women could call attention to what is happening in Tibet and to the plight of Tibetans outside their homeland.'

'So how does the Miss Tibet contest work?'

'We have a website and contestants can log in and send us their details. In our first year, 2000, we got thirty applications. Of which ten contestants turned up to meet us, and finally four girls showed up for the event. One girl was a school dropout, one a kindergarten teacher and two were from a college in the US. It was all very new to the girls as we have several rounds—introduction, interview, swimsuit, evening gown, talent round, question and answer round, traditional costume round. The crowning is done in traditional Tibetan attire. The whole thing spans over three days. The first year the BBC was most intrigued and reported our contest and interviewed me. We had non-Tibetan judges and we marked our presence and raised our voice through the platform of beauty by crowning Miss Tibet.'

Both Anand and Mohini were intrigued, 'And what of Miss Tibet after her selection?'

'Miss Tibet has gone on to participate in the Miss Asia Pacific and Miss Earth pageants in the Philippines. Of course, every place Miss Tibet goes, Miss China has always come and insisted that she is Miss Tibet.' Lobsang smiled, 'Miss Tibet gets to draw attention to the Tibetans and our cause. Miss Tibet 2007, Tenzin Dolma, has done very well as a ramp model.'

While they were sipping tea, Mohini turned to him, 'Did you have sponsors?'

'Yes. People help out in different ways. In the year 2014 there was a documentary made on the contest called 'Miss Tibet: Beauty in Exile' that premiered in the Documentary Film Festival in New York. While it assuaged some curiosity about the Tibetans in exile it didn't bring in as many sponsors for the event as we had hoped. The money was always an issue as it was never enough for holding the pageant every year. The prize money for Miss Tibet is one lakh rupees, and the only year I was comfortable was 2017. The upcoming Miss Tibet 2018 will be held in New York. In fact I am travelling to New York to go over the details with my partners.'

'So are you outsourcing it?'

'Something like that…I have been doing it for such a long time, it's time for a change. I will always be the proprietor, but my partners will run it. I want to start a new Miss Himalaya Contest that gives opportunity to young women from Ladakh to Arunachal Pradesh—the entire mountain belt.'

'That's very ambitious,' Anand said.

Lobsang grinned, raising his tea cup as a toast, 'Yah, it is. But then we will never know how we fare till we try it. We are talking about it 30,000 feet in the air, who knows what other new beginnings will start when we touchdown?'

Mariko

HEADS TURN AS I enter Green Cafe. Outside the drizzle has started and my hair and wrap have caught a few drops. I run my fingers through my hair and my reflection catches the long floor-to-ceiling mirror that lines one wall of the cafe. I like what I see. A tall oriental woman with a taut body and shoulder-length blonde hair, stylishly attired, with a deep maroon pout to die for.

The cafe is crowded, His Holiness is giving his teachings the next day and the town has suddenly come alive with outsiders. I ignore the lull in the conversation and the watchful eyes of the cafe crowd and walk towards the unknown woman who wants to interview me. She is sitting watching the Dhauladhar range playing hide-and-seek with the clouds. It's a perfect evening in McLeod Ganj, Dharamshala, the kind when the rain lends it a perfect romance.

'Mariko,' she stands, saying my name aloud. I smile. Her eyes widen taking me in. We shake hands. She looks at my manicured nails in admiration. She is a pleasant looking woman with dyed hair that doesn't fully hide the white that peeps at the roots, dressed in a blue men's shirt, jeans and sneakers. I have always wondered why women want to underplay their looks.

Mariko

She leads me to the secluded part of the open terrace where a table awaits us, its checked tablecloth framed against the backdrop of flamboyant begonias in tall pots. A camera has been set up and a bearded man is fiddling with the focus. Beards are really in these days, I think, or maybe men are just too lazy to shave. Tibetan men have less facial hair which mostly centres in the middle of the chin and grows like straggly goat tails. I am lucky I didn't have to undergo electrolysis. There is nothing efficient waxing can't fix.

'Ready?' the camera man asks. I hold up my phone with its wide screen—my reflection looks alright. I shake my hair out. If I am to appear on Buzz Word I might as well look groomed.

'What does Mariko mean?'

I smile. It's a question that I am always asked. She watches me, her eyes widening as she takes in how the smile transforms my face. If you asked me to pick my best feature, I would say my lips—wide, generous, sensuous. My friends tell me that I get more selfie requests than His Holiness. Of course I laugh it off as a joke between friends because even to say it aloud in conservative Tibetan society is blasphemy.

I take a sip of the coffee, which is frothy and warm. The conversation has lulled in the surrounding tables and I ignore it. I know they are talking about me. Chances are they are listening in. It happens all the time. I shrug, cupping the white china, revelling in its warmth. 'There is a Rinpoche who goes very often to teach in Japan, so I asked him if he could suggest a new name, some very

Japanese style name to the one my parents gave me, so he wrote a name out on a sheet of paper and gave it to me. I slept with it under my pillow and the more I said it aloud, the more I loved it, so I took it up.'

'What was the name you were born with?'

'Tenzin Ugen.' I smile, 'That was twenty years ago.'

'Start from the beginning,' she says.

I am effervescent as I am supposed to be in my new avatar, relaying the story of my transformation from being a monk to becoming transgender. I play along, answering the questions thrown at me. These days when I close my eyes, even for a fraction of a second, I see a shadow detach itself and move away to stand at the sidelines. I am there, yet I am not there at all. A part of me is always a bystander. I have been interviewed so many times and almost always it's the same line of questioning—everyone looking for an answer for how I became a transgender. The first woman interviewer, an American who interviewed me after I had danced in the Miss Tibet pageant, had described my transformation as 'emerging from a chrysalis to become a butterfly'. I had laughed but it had chafed because I was no butterfly, however exotic my species was.

Half an hour later it's a wrap. We shake hands and I move away. Outside the sidewalks are full of tourists, more are arriving for tomorrow's sermons—the world seeking the reason for being.

Soft rain begins to fall as I walk home, my heels making a steady tattoo on the cobbled streets all the way uphill and then sloping down to Amdo village. For nearly sixty years my people have lived in this village as refugees. The familiar names of Tibet given to settlements are the only reminders of our homeland. Once our parents roamed free on the vast plains of the wild, untamed land proclaimed as the roof of the world. Now they live in homes built back to back, one on top of the other, cramped in a few acres of exile in McLeod. Two generations of Tibetans are growing up here clinging on to stories their grandparents tell.

The door is open and I can hear the television blaring an old Bollywood film, which means Pala is home. I can hear my brothers Sonam and Tashi busy in the kitchen, it's their turn to cook. Pala's eyes follow me stonily as I walk to the room that I share with Tashi. His silence is deafening. When I first came out, his abuses were endless and he even beat me, Now his angry tirade that I had become the community's laughing stock has stopped. It's as if I don't exist. Pala's one angry hiss every time he raised his hand on me would be: 'I fathered five sons. Five. I don't know you and I don't know what you have become.' But at the drop of a hat this silent veneer would crack up as he joked and laughed with my siblings. Since I became trans, he has never included me.

I sit in front of a mirror and slowly remove my make-up, following the step-by-step method I learnt from my style icon Alessandra Ambrosio, a top model of Victoria's Secret fame. At the Green Cafe with its free Wi-Fi, I used to sit with my phone watching her style and make-up tips for hours on end. The first time Pala saw me with my make-up on, he had gritted his teeth and spat out 'Whore!' before walking out. I had swallowed my tears and locked myself in my room. I don't know whether that was in shame or sorrow.

That night I had woken up to see Pala in our room watching me sleep. Sitting by the window on the lone chair with the street light falling on him, he looked grey, defeated and very old. When had Pala turned so old? I had felt my heart squeeze at his plight. We were on two sides of a river whose depth we didn't know. He left around dawn, as silently as he had come.

I tie my shoulder-length hair into a top knot, carefully put away my clothes, pull on a loose T-shirt and track pants, wash my face and walk to the kitchen. The others are sitting around a square table. Pala has as usual taken his food to the living room, where he sleeps ever since he and Amala divorced. He has moved the family altar above the television and spends hours reading the holy scriptures, meditating or telling his beads.

We sit around and eat. Sonam works as a cook in Hotel Tibet and when it's his day to cook he prefers to cook Indian as throughout the day he is cooking Tibetan or Chinese meals. Today we have dal-bhaat and seasonal vegetables with lots of salad. Sonam is an effortless cook, he always said Amala taught him when he was little. My brothers eat with gusto while I use a fork and eat slowly, chewing just as models tell you to. The boys no longer make fun of me—they accept that I have to keep my figure. In heels I stand at 6 feet and 2 inches; I know I stand out anywhere. Given my genes, if I am not careful, I can easily become broad-shouldered and beefy. I need to keep myself willowy instead of sinewy.

I volunteer to do the dishes and make tea. The boys settle down to playing carrom—it's noisy and Pala has raised the decibel of the television even louder. They are fighting for the queen and I stand grinning at the palpable excitement. The only one missing in this excitement is the queen herself, Amala.

Amala, with her long thick raven black hair and the delicate arched eyebrows that framed an animated face. The corner of her lips always tilted upwards ready to smile. Her gentle touch and soft crooning voice surrounded us in a net of loving care. Amala had told us when we were little that she and Pala had married under trying circumstances, eking out a bare existence on a vast government farm. Born in Tibet under the Chinese they only spoke Chinese. Amongst themselves they whispered endearments in Tibetan at night.

Their grandparents had taught them the language in whispers and told them all about the Dalai Lama whom they adored. To mention his name aloud was to get imprisoned for life. Pala and Amala had only one ambition: to come to McLeod Ganj to be with the Dalai Lama and raise their children under his shadow. Taking along their four children on the pretext of a pilgrimage, they made the arduous journey to India as late as 1992. When they reached McLeod they never went back. There was nothing to go back to. They never talked of their life in Tibet. It was as if they had wiped it clean, along with every bitter unhappy memory. Pala got a job in the Tibetan Children's School and Amala worked wherever she could to supplement the family income. A year later I was born, and three years later Tashi.

Having worked on the farm, Amala could grow just

about anything anywhere. Our small patch in Bir had squashes, pumpkins, gourds, maize and spinach. I would trail her everywhere and play with her lipstick, powders, eye pencil and nail polish. Amala would hug me when I tottered around in her sandals, calling me her little boy-girl.

I look around, it has been years since Amala left and without her the house has lost its sheen. Pala sits with his legs propped up on the centre table, dressed in shorts and a T-shirt. He looks like an aging footballer running to fat. The raucous betting does not disturb him. There is an air of detachment that wasn't there earlier. He has taken down the lone family photo from the mantlepiece where it had been put up by Amala. I keep it in my room as a relic of our happier times.

It is a black-and-white photo of Amala with turquoise in her hair seated on a chair, behind which Pala stands in his traditional chuba. Behind them are draped two archlike curtains giving a sense of grandeur. Amala is holding Tashi on her lap, a mere baby of three months. We all stand around positioned by the photographer according to our order of birth. While Sonam is standing erect by Pala's side I am leaning against Amala. She is the only one smiling in the photo. It's as if she held the key to the family's happiness, very like the Indian folktale she told us where the soul of the magician rested in a parrot. To kill him was to kill the parrot. Amala was that parrot. With her gone the soul had flown from our family.

Pala and Amala fought, and sometimes it was bitter and full of recrimination. Then one day after Tashi turned three, Pala told us he was taking us for lunch. We skipped and walked past rows of shops selling trinkets, amulets and beads, past shops that sold hand-painted thankas and spiritual books, past all the old and new cafes. Pala took us to Hotel Amdo, perched atop a hill, that provided cheap food and a fantastic view. He said we could order anything and we took a menu each. Not that I could read much, being just six. So I ordered my favourite chicken thukpa. Amala just had a cup of tea. When we had finished, Pala looked around, cleared his throat and said he and Amala had an announcement to make: 'Amala and I have decided to divorce. You all will stay with me and Amala will not live with us anymore.'

'For how long?' I had asked.

'Forever,' Amala had said. We were all stunned. Pala had been strict and had often hit us as punishment while Amala never did. But that day as she sat there seeming carved out of stone, without uttering a word, it was the most painful slap to us. We sat there not knowing what to do. Pala and Amala had their faces set, as if they were already divorced. The next day Amala was gone.

Thank god I had the family photo. It was my only reminder of Amala. When she left there was no trace of her, no clothes, no powder or eye pencil. No scent of the fresh junipers that she always smelt of.

After she left, Pala was like a man in a daze. He would be up early, cooking before going to work. The house was a mess. Everything was covered in a layer of dust, and we barely managed. Pala would leave home with his tiffin carrying Tashi while we went to school. Amala's garden patch wilted from neglect. We barely managed to keep our heads up. It was the start of more things to come.

That summer Pala's relatives from Darjeeling came visiting. They were watchful of all the goings-on in the house and full of advice. During the school summer vacations, Pala announced that he was taking me and Tashi for a holiday. We had friends who would tell us of their holidays, and now for the first time we would have something to tell our friends. Amidst great excitement Pala took us by bus to Delhi and from there we took a train to Darjeeling. Tashi and I were thrilled, counting stations and watching the milling crowds. Even Pala was lighthearted and bought lollipops and sticky boiled sweets for us from stations. It took us two whole nights to reach Jalpaiguri. From there we took a tourist jeep to Darjeeling.

By the time we reached Darjeeling, the snowy peaks of Kanchenjunga were lit up in golden hues. Pala led us to a monastery. 'We are going to stay here for the night.' It was the Kagyu Karma Tashi monastery. We had dinner and slept. The next day he took us to town. It was fun, we walked the Chowrasta and ate food at a restaurant. Then he led us to have our heads shaved. Since Amala left, he had started tonsuring our heads. That evening there were maroon robes lying on the bed.

'Come on, change up,' Pala called out, already changing Tashi.

'I don't want to be a monk. I am not changing,' I yelled. 'You can't force me.'

Pala was angry, he slapped me. 'Both of you are becoming monks, is that understood?'

I shook my head, tears coursing down my cheeks, so Pala changed his tone saying it was what he wanted for us. We would get food and be looked after. He made sure I changed and then tucked us in, telling us stories till we fell asleep. The next morning when we woke up Pala was gone.

It was frightening. A new place full of strangers. We clung together, our eyes glued to the monastery gates hoping Pala would come back, but he never did. We only knew Tibetan and everyone spoke Nepali. At play time the boys would run around with a football, yelling and calling out in Nepali. I was ten and Tashi was seven. I became his caregiver. Thank god we had each other. We had no way to contact Pala, no phone number and no address. So there was no way back.

Slowly the monastery became a home. We would be up early like the other monks, wash up and rush for studies, our voices rising and falling like a steady drone of bees, soothing and full of worship. We learnt all our prayers by rote and like a sponge drew in all the lessons and teachings. It was a good regimented life since we followed fixed timetables. Pala never came back to Darjeeling but once a year he would meet us at Bodh Gaya when the monks took all the novices for the Kagyu Monlam—that was when hundreds of monks from all disciplines of Tibetan Buddhism came together in Bodh Gaya to offer prayers in the place where the Buddha attained enlightenment. It was held every year in December or January. Slowly, being a monk became a way of life.

The front door closes with a loud bang startling me. The constant rain has warped the wood and the latch only closes after you have pulled it with all your strength. I can hear the patter of rain on the tin roof. The rounds of carrom have ended. Tashi walks in yawning and asks, 'How was your day?'

'Okay. An interview with Buzz Word and then I walked home. I also got a call today from *Elle* and they want to shoot me for their eleventh anniversary edition. They are calling it 'Icons.''

'Wow. Sounds impressive.' He lies down, pulling on the covers. The rain beats a steady tattoo on the roof. I put the photograph away and lie down tucking the warm blanket around me. We are facing each other on our twin beds, separated by the table that holds our books and a table lamp. Tashi has a far-off look. He is the closest to me, unquestioning and always agreeable.

'Tenzin, may I ask you something?'

I look at him askance; he is scary when he begins like this. It means he has played it out in his mind a lot. He clears his throat. 'Tenzin, are you happy? Really happy?'

I grin, he knows I get a kick coming out in the media and being heralded as a Tibetan queer icon.

'Does it not bother you that people see you as queer? Isn't that an English word for strange? Can you continue to live a life as a queer till you die? What if you decide some years down the line that this transgender business was because you were confused?'

I look at him, but he avoids my gaze. I can guess that my brothers have talked. I understand that they worry and are still getting used to the changes in my world. 'Confused? Yes, I know that what is not known or understood is queer. But Tashi, I am very happy for coming out as trans.'

'Trans for a lifetime?'

'Yes. Why are you asking me this again when we have been through this before?'

His eyes are sombre, 'Will you be okay, really okay?'

'Yes. What's there to not be okay? I know I never shared it before but I was restless inside, only I could not articulate what left me dissatisfied. Monkhood teaches you not to have expectations. I had none but often I felt hollow inside. Although I was taught the meaning of life but strangely, I was always seeking the reason of my being. Now I know who I am and finally am at peace.'

'I don't know how to say this, but I want you to be happy. But I also don't want you to be queer.' Tashi's seventeen-year-old face is solemn as he faces me. Our sister Dolma too had said the same thing. Married at eighteen, she lived in the cantonment of Dharamshala in an army colony. Her only worry was that I should not be seen as abnormal, that I should live a stable normal life. It was in her home that I had sought refuge in when I first came out. I avoided the family because of their murderous rage when I became a woman. For months McLeod was a hub of Chinese whispers, with everyone talking of the monk who had gone mad and was dressing up as a woman. They had run my background through inside out, creating a debris of opinion. It brought to the fore the unspoken cultural gap that exists between the first wave of immigrants who came with His Holiness and raised Indian-born Tibetans, in comparison to later immigrants who came from Chinese-occupied Tibet and were dismissed as 'Byor Pa' or newcomers. That my parents came in as late as 1992, had been born in Chinese-overrun Tibet, spoke Mandarin, watched Chinese films and could sing Chinese songs meant that they were half-breeds. My wild behaviour was the fall-out of all that.

My transition tarred the younger generation of Tibetans as a generation that was forgetting their ways and becoming too modern, flaunting themselves, blurring sexual lines and bringing a bad name to the community. That's when I left being a monk. My Rinpoche said, 'You can't abuse the robe—leave and do what you want with your life.'

I sigh. Tashi's inquisition reminds me of the volley of poison that had been unleashed when I had just wanted to be myself. I had cried for days as if my tears were penance. I just felt as a woman deep inside and wanted to live that, celebrate it. Dolma said that in olden days they would have stoned me to death. Not that the barbs and snide remarks were less than stones. The words of disdain and ridicule tore at me when I was alone at night and made me cry.

'Tashi, you have been speaking to people, isn't it? I know that within the Tibetan community I am still a freak who dragged the community centrestage with my transition. I know no Tibetan born anywhere as a man had dressed as a woman and decided to live life as a transgender. I know I have dragged the community into the gender and sexuality debate and that this is shocking for a community which is headed by a monk. But people aren't one-dimensional. None of us choose the world we are born in. I didn't either. For a long time, I felt strange feelings inside me... like I was a refugee living in a no man's land. I was waiting to find the guts to come out and feel whole.'

Tashi is quiet. 'Are you whole?'

'Yes, oh yes. Now. I am very happy. I am not living a pretense anymore.'

'But Tenzin, what about the sex change? Will you do it?' He looks at me anxiously. We have had this conversation once before when I had started dressing trans.

I turn my head away. I don't tell him that on my last visit to Delhi I had gone to a doctor at the bustling Lajpat Nagar market. A man with shifty eyes and a nervous smile had examined me physically and asked numerous questions before prescribing hormones. I had taken a week of hormone injections from him and then been on oral pills. It's funny how hormones play on your body and mind. He had tried to warn me, but nothing he said prepared me for the funny pop and tingling that would grip me at unexpected places. I can feel a prickling in my breasts and butt, that have become more rounded. Each time I stand in front of the mirror after my bath I can see the changes. My skin is softer and more prone to sensation; there is a smoothness in my face that had not been there. The only one to notice was my friend Norbu: 'Tenzin you have become so girl-like—even the way you blush when people pay you compliments is like a real girl. I really think your breasts are now real too.' I had blushed and looked away, hiding from his astute eyes.

But that night when everyone slept, I stood in the bathroom with my T-shirt off, staring at my breasts. They were no longer flat, they had risen and peaked like soft crested mounds.

The house is quiet and a watery moon splays our room with light. I cannot sleep. I think back to the time when we were at the Kagyu Monlam in Bodh Gaya. We had been transferred from Darjeeling to Kathmandu to another monastery from where I was to sit for my high school exams. We had been walking down the crowded street with the rest when I saw a woman who looked hauntingly familiar. Tashi and I stood by the roadside, unmindful of the jostling crowd, to watch her. Twenty minutes later we stepped up to the small stall where she was selling shafahlay and noodles.

She was busy attending to people and frying at the same time. The smell of fried meat permeated the air.

'Amala?'

She looked at me and nodded in polite inquiry, 'Inchinla?'

All women her age are called Amala.

'Amala. It's me, Tenzin, and look, this is Tashi.'

For a while her polite unseeing eyes were deadpan, staring at me and then at Tashi, then something stirred in their ebony depths and created a forest fire. She yelled as she came bounding out of the small stall to hug the two of us, kissing and holding us in a tight embrace. She closed shop soon after, cooking and feeding us instead. The tears never stopped flowing. We were meeting after five years.

Monkhood teaches you detachment but nothing can take the place of a mother. We clung to her every word and revelled in her embrace. She still smelt of fresh juniper. The days together with Amala were fun-filled. We had so much to catch up on. She gave us money so I could buy a cell phone and the very first number I recorded was Amala's. We helped out at her stall and every evening she would sit with us and we would talk incessantly. It was the best Monlam ever.

When we left for Kathmandu by bus, she was there to see us off. She held me tight saying we will meet again, and stepped away. Tashi and I could talk of nothing else but Amala.

'I wish we could run away,' Tashi said, midway to our journey. Villages rushed by and he looked at me with such hope. I turned away so that he could not see the same glint in my eyes.

Unwittingly he had sown the seed that had never been there. Meeting Amala was like being inundated with all the wistfulness that we had thought had been consigned to our lost childhood. But it had returned with bigger hunger and longing. Amala represented a whole, and not the scattered bits our lives had become. How could we search for salvation when she represented it?

Exactly three months later, Tashi and I made our way to the bus terminal with two thousand Nepali rupees. We had scraped together everything we owned. But the cost of one ticket from Kathmandu to Delhi was two thousand rupees. We were stuck, so we begged the ticket collector and the bus driver to take us. I even said I would make Tashi sit on my lap. Ultimately they allowed both of us to sit in the driver's cabin. Luck works in strange ways. An army man from 22 Establishment gave us food. When we reached Delhi he took us to their camp for the night, and the next day he bought our tickets to Dharamshala.

At home I faced the brunt of Pala's anger. Pala could not for the life of him imagine how we could run away from the monastery and that too not from Darjeeling but Nepal. He was at his wits' end trying to get us back to the monastery at the earliest. We still wore monk robes and went for teachings but other than that we stayed home.

In a way Tashi and I were monks without any destination. Pala tried his best to get us into a monastery but we had also made him guilty of abandonment so that he didn't pursue it too hard. But father was old-school; he felt leaving his boys with free time meant inviting trouble so he appealed to all his friends to look for jobs or volunteering opportunities for them. Unexpectedly through the Rinpoche I got the opportunity to work as a volunteer at the Tibetan Chamber of Commerce in Delhi. Being in the capital city was exciting so I went willingly.

The Chief Co-Ordinator Sonam La became a good friend. After office hours I would try all the make-up tricks I had learnt from YouTube on her. She was all set to get married and leave for America so I helped her buy her trousseau. It was while we shopped that I once told her it was my deepest desire to dress as a woman in an evening gown.

'Do it,' she urged, and being together with a friend in vast Delhi made me more courageous. We shopped for a long wig and a flame orange robe that I wore for her wedding reception, dolling up with all the make-up tricks I had learnt. I loved every minute of it. I danced a lot and enjoyed myself. What I didn't realize was that people were taking videos of the party. Someone put a video of me dancing on WeChat, which went viral. Even before I reached McLeod Ganj, I had a horde of people wanting to know if I had dressed like a woman and danced at a wedding. I was scared by all the attention and the outrage, so I lied. I denied everything and took refuge in Dolma's house.

Dolma was two years older to me and she warded off Pala and the boys as best as she could. But it was to Amala that she turned for help. Amala lived in McLeod. She had her own partner now as did Pala. They had both moved on in life. Amala still possessed the uncanny ability to deal with crisis best.

When Dolma brought in Amala I could not hold on any longer and I told her everything. Amala heard me, her calm face changing to surprise, then anger and utter dismay.

'Tenzin, you are confused—let's visit the Lama who does Mo and can predict, it could be you are possessed and that is why you are behaving so strangely. You have lost your shadow.'

I looked at my mother. What she said made me stop short—a man without a shadow is frightening. But I was sure she was saying all of this in distress. 'Amala, I will never go for Mo. I am fine. I beg you to listen to me.'

'Did you feel this way when you were a monk?'

'I felt something. While my friends would look at cars and things like that, I would look at women and their make-up. I wanted to be like them. Even then I tweezed my eyebrows, applied Vaseline. I was the monk with the shiniest lips.'

Amala caught my hand and turned it around, noting that my nails had been meticulously filed and painted shell pink. 'Amala, I have finally found myself.'

'As a man who dresses like a woman. What work will you do? How will you feed yourself?'

'I will work,' I mumbled. Even I was not clear about what I would do.

'Men who dress as women end up as prostitutes,' her eyes teared up,

'No,' I shook my head. 'I won't bring shame to the family, I promise you that. The years of my monkhood will never be in vain.' She held me fiercely as she ran her hand down my back and soothed my tears.

It was a beginning. Amala was the one who brought in Pala after talking to him. All he did was sit and watch me without saying anything. I knew he felt ashamed of me. He left wordlessly, without a backward glance. My brothers didn't help either; their open contempt at seeing me in women's clothes was like a knife that left me bleeding. Only Tashi stayed with me.

I knew my life would be unconventional, but *how* unconventional—I had no idea. Then I got an unexpected call from Lobsang Wangyal, the organizer of the Miss Tibet beauty contest; he approached me to find out if I was interested in dancing for them. Already they were facing flak from the community for toying with a western concept of commodifying women through the beauty pageant. The community was divided: the young insisted that they had to move with time, while the more conventional elders felt it went against their Tibetan-ness and their traditional ethos. The raging debate would remain unresolved and would always divide the community. The organizers insisted that the only way ahead was to move with the times.

I aped the line. It defined me as well. I agreed to work for the pageant.

I didn't tell the family; they would know soon enough. The decision to work for the pageant had also made me think of how I could become an entertainer with a difference—a dancer, style icon and a role model for those who wanted to be like me but were afraid and still in the closet. I felt I was ready. My years of discipline as a monk were what I would hold on to diligently. I was determined that I would be an all-round artiste. It would be my way of giving back to the community.

Already in its second year, Miss Tibet was being televised by the cable operators in McLeod. The idea was novel and it excited the youth. Banners across town were getting lot of attention, and not just curious tourists but indeed the whole town was agog.

The stage was set on the outskirts of McLeod as people crowded around the lone football stadium lit by floodlights. The stadium was entirely full, and the crowd exceeded the wildest imagination of the organizers. I could taste the anticipation in the air. The two-day pageant had already moved from the prelims, heading for its grand finale.

'Mariko, you ready? We are pulling out our wild card now,' the emcee asked me.

I gave him a thumbs up sign. I was too nervous to say anything. He nodded and moved onto the lighted stage, his amplified voice booming, 'Tashi delek, ladies and gentlemen,' in Tibetan, welcoming the cheering crowd, 'We now have a special number before our grand finale, just for you—and it's Marikoooo!'

The strains of 'Aap Jaisa Koi Nahi' rent the air and I step into the white lights. The woofers are booming as I twirl effortlessly and move further into the light, my skirt billowing. The crowd surges forward and their screams wash over me like waves. They are calling out my name: 'Mariko, Mariko!' The screams have the effect of adrenaline. This moment is mine. The strains of the song reach a crescendo as I turn to take my final bow and turn away from the light. I see it then—my shadow—it's very much there, right beside me.

I have metamorphosed. I have finally found my path. The internet is jammed with over 85,000 views of a Tibetan queer idol, a dancer, an entertainer and a youth icon. My phone hasn't stopped ringing with requests for photoshoots and interviews.

I am on the other side now.

I am finally Mariko—the Truth—the name the Rinpoche gave to me.

RED
Fire

The Medal

'Popo-la, you were in the army?'

Jayang looked up from the newspaper, frowning. His ten-year-old grandson Tsering's incredulous eyes were on his old photo album, aflame with excitement at the discovery. A box of dog tags, rank badges, service accoutrements and berets lay open along with his grandfather's service file.

'Popo-la, I can't believe it, you never told me, no one told me.' He was holding up a photo, 'Popo-la, is this you?'

Jayang walked up to him and sat down on the floor. He took the photo and squinted at the black-and-white group picture of men in jump rigs strapped with parachutes, framed besides an Avro aircraft. Young strapping men smiling at the camera that had captured the adrenaline flush all jumpers have before they jump off among the clouds.

Jayang pushed his glasses back and sat for a long while looking at the photo. He was right in the middle of the group and was surprised Tsering had pointed him out. He could almost hear his teacher saying, 'Age may change you but it can never take the five-year-old boy out of you, he will always peep out of you… and if you look hard, he will always be there.'

He grinned, still looking at the photo. It was almost a lifetime ago—Agra, where they trained to become the first airborne Tibetan force of the 22 Establishment, headquartered in Chakrata, some hundred miles away from the lush Dehra valley framed by jagged blue hills.

He bent down and pulled out the album from the black tin trunk that had his name, Jayang Chhering, painted on it. He smiled at another photo of himself with a comrade, both freshly bald, in dungarees, holding rifles and running up an incline. It was their first cross-country run. One of the instructors had been clicking pictures. He had given it to him and another one to Samphel. Just looking at the photo, Jayang could feel the harsh breath, the sweat and the smell of pine forests. Nothing mattered except the tricolour that flew at the finish point of the run.

A soldier was the last thing Jayang expected to become. He was just five when his parents had sent him off to the Sera monastery in Lhasa. For fifteen years he had led the life of a monk. He had followed in the wake of multitudes fleeing in chaos and panic to India, then aged twenty-two, to find himself rootless and directionless.

To fit into his new life, instead of a monastery he was enrolled in school in Dharamshala. It felt strange to be in a classroom with ten-year-olds learning English alphabets and basic grammar. His classmates nicknamed him and his friend Samphel, who was of the same age, as the Popo-las' of Class Five. The first time he heard them call him grandfather he had laughed till his stomach hurt and the class had joined in. They weren't far from the truth. He and Samphel stuck out like giants—like the ones in the colourful story book *Gulliver's Travels*, among his Lilliputian classmates.

One day the school had strange visitors. They were rough-looking men wearing the old fashioned Tibetan chuba and knee-high boots, their long hair tied back in a plait in red silk. Their leader addressed the older students: 'Tashi delek, everyone. We are looking for volunteers, young men who will join the Tibetan army that the Indian government wants to raise.'

It was November of 1962 and the India-China war had ended a month back. A humiliating defeat for India had it smarting as China had overrun the Indian defences as far as Bomdila, right up to Chaku in Missamari where the Tibetan refugee camp had been set up in 1959. The Tibetans had heard it all on the radio and in newspapers; the talk of China was incessant. The man addressing the school assembly had ended his speech by reiterating the Indian government's decision to raise an army of Tibetans to fight the Chinese and win back Tibet. The Dalai Lama had given his approval to the plan.

Jayang felt his heart thudding. He had finally found a light in his dark tunnel, a path—fighting for his homeland.

He wasn't alone, there was a long line of young men like him who enlisted. Bundled into waiting army trucks they raced to Pathankot, staying the night there and then making a convoy to reach a camp in Dehradun. The next halt was Chakrata.

Jayang stepped out of the truck to see the place swarming with Tibetan men—it was as if everyone wanted to join the army. There was palpable excitement in the boisterous camaraderie that filled the camp, almost as if each man could smell the pungent Tibetan soil and feel the cold mountain air that had never left his soul.

The next day, over 2000 of them were divided into groups and sent to the military hospital in Dehra for checkups. The medicals were stringent, like separating the wheat from the chaff. Jayang sailed through without a glitch, as did Samphel. When they returned to camp, more trucks rolled in carrying fresh batches of Tibetan youth, all hung up on becoming soldiers for their homeland.

That was when their training started in earnest. It was punishing. Up at four, they would run cross country, up steep gradients, building strength and endurance. They barely knew when the sun rose and when it was lights out; they were on the move all the time. Within a month of the training, the men had turned lean and supple. The outdoor training was followed by map reading and survival skills in high altitude areas. By the end of the third month they were taken to Agra for their parajumps. They were being trained to become high altitude warriors who knew how to jump out of an aircraft and had skills to survive in cold desolate places.

The first time that Jayang jumped off an aircraft, his breath caught in his throat and his stomach opened up. He closed his eyes as the wind tore at him and the land appeared like a distant patch of green; fear made his heartbeat sound like crashing waves. Months of being drilled forced him to look at his altometer and pull his parachute cord well in time to land safely. The subsequent jumps were easier and more thrilling. After seven basic jumps he was commandeered to pack the parachutes (the main and the reserve), a job of great precision as in his packing rested the life of every man. Painstakingly precise, he made sure he never faltered. He also learnt how to prepare free drops of rations and heavy artillery guns. Everything he learnt thrilled him as it was a new skill.

Ten months later he passed out and became a sepoy of the Special Frontier Force (SFF). He was sent back to Agra as Jump Master to train young recruits for para jumps and free falls. He loved free falling, just stepping off the aircraft at over 20,000 feet and gliding in the sky like a bird till he fell to a certain height, pulled the parachute chord and manoeuvred himself to the ground.

When the 1965 India-Pakistan war broke out, Jayang had moved after a three-year stint as Jump Master from the Agra Para Centre to the Aviation Research Centre (ARC), Sarsawa, in the hinterland of Uttar Pradesh. Hidden from any habitation by acres of sugarcane fields, the ARC was a training centre and airbase of the Indian intelligence agency innocuously called the Research and Analysis Wing or just RAW. It was RAW that had raised the Tibetans to be a secret high-altitude guerrilla warrior force, to carry out covert operations behind Chinese lines, especially if there was another Sino-Indian war.

It was easy to love the life of a soldier—the camaraderie, the constant action-oriented schedules, the para jumps and free falls into the velvet darkness guided by maps and instinct. Among themselves they would constantly talk of when they would face the enemy. They were ready. They started badgering their Director General (DG),

Major General S.S. Uban, an ex-Indian army officer who had commanded the 22 Mountain Division in the Second World War and been awarded the Military Cross. The DG would raise his hand and say, 'When the time is right, we will celebrate Losar in Lhasa, I promise.'

By 1971 the Indian sub-continent was in turmoil, with the Pakistani government engaged in quelling the liberation movement of the Bengali population in East Pakistan. The Bengali freedom fighters had formed a resistance force, calling themselves 'Mukti Bahini.' Their political party, Awami League, had won a landslide victory but their demand for separation from Pakistan had led to the Pakistani army suppressing all resistance. There was a mass exodus of Bengalis seeking refuge in India.

Rumours that war between India and Pakistan was imminent abounded. It was early November of 1971 when the SFF's Tibetan leaders were asked if they would take part in the war that was threatening to start between India and Pakistan. The leaders had sought the Dalai Lama's counsel and had been given his blessings. The Dalai Lama had said, 'They gave us shelter, now it's our turn to reciprocate.'

Jayang still had a photo of that time. Wearing his olive greens and holding a rifle, with a loaded backpack, one in a company of men grinning at the camera.

'Which place is this, where are you all going?' little Tsering asked.

Jayang picked up the picture and said, 'To war.'

'You fought a war? A real war?' Jayang watched his grandson's eyes become round orbs. 'For Tibet, Popo-la?'

Jayang nodded, recalling the day they headed for the

border. 'It was the fourth of November 1971, we were in Chakrata, our headquarters where we Tibetans had been recruited to the Special Frontier Force to fight for Tibet. But the war we went into was not against the Chinese… it was against Pakistan. It was our first operation since we had been raised.

'The Dalai Lama had given his approval for action. Early morning, we were taken by trucks from Chakrata to Sarsawa. That night we boarded a Dakota aircraft and reached Silchar in Assam. The next day we travelled up to Damagari in Mizoram, where the 22 Establishment had its base and hospital. Then at Lunglei on the India-East Pakistan border we camped for six days, practicing ambush and guerrilla tactics, awaiting further orders.

'We were six companies each of about 120 men, divided into the north, south and central columns. I was in the south column as its Assault Party Commander. I had 110 men under me. The other companies were our reserve and the support company. One company was tasked to put up a road block on the Burma road which we felt would be used by the enemy to escape.

'Our D-Day was the thirteenth of November, 1971. At six in the evening, the Commanding Officer Sahib shook my hand and said, "Jayang good luck. Jeet ke aana." We walked into the jungle following two lungi-clad men that the BSF had got for us as guides. The forest was dense; within minutes we were wading through neck deep swamps, staying concealed in the marshes. By 10 p.m. we reached Jailenpari, a Pakistani camp. Our local intel had the enemy head count at 150 Pakistani army regulars,

150 Mizos and 100 Razakars. Our time to attack was 4 a.m. on fourteenth November.

'The Pakistani camp was heavily fortified and booby-trapped. Throughout the night we went around removing the mines. When I asked our guides to go a little closer to the Pakistani camp, trip wire flares placed by the enemy lighted up. The trip flares light up when you cross wires that are zig-zagged on the jungle floor, giving off a bright volley of fire. The sentries called out a warning and our guides ran away thrashing into the forest.

'Using the radio, I called up our CO Sahib and told him we were ready for the attack. He told us to wait for the enemy to fire first. Sure enough, the sentries let out a volley of shots—but they were all directed towards the front of the camp. The guides had smartly led us to the rear of the camp which we had now surrounded.

'We began firing our mortars and machine guns. On our flanks our support company too started giving us supporting fire. I stood up then and all my men stood alongside in the exploding fireworks. We rushed into the cacophony of firing shouting, "AIIIIIEEEEEEE!" It was a loud ancient war cry of over a hundred men, and the forest reverberated with it. It stopped the enemy for a while. The enemy prisoners later told us that our war cry was different to the ones used by the Indian army and hence they were confused as to who was attacking them,' Tshering laughed aloud as Jayang paused, grinning at the memory. 'I am sure we Tibetans had the same war cry centuries ago when we fought and defeated the Chinese.

'There was a deafening burst of machine gun fire.

Bombs were falling and bullets were flying around. I yelled for the men to stay on the ground and not stand as the firing was intense. Those who heard me crouched and slithered towards the enemy, firing in crouching position. Despite our yelling to hit the ground, our young sepoys, who had just finished recruit training and had joined afresh, were hit.

'I stood up when I saw my boys take a hit and still in that crouched position ran ahead. The firing was intense and already I could see the enemy was fleeing. Men were running wrapped in bedsheets—they had no time to wear their pants. My radio operator was alongside. Just as we neared the built-up area, the radio operator took a hit, crumpled and fell. He lay twitching, blood oozing from his chest, the radio still strapped to his back. I ran towards him and got hit by a bullet in my leg. The pain was excruciating as I dragged him to safety. When I lay beside him, I saw he was dead. My head was spinning and my leg was on fire. We all carried medical kits, and someone injected me with morphine. Within a little time I felt better. I kept directing my men and we cleared the area. When the last shot stopped, we did a head count. We had lost eight men and twelve had been injured, including me. The Pakistani side had many dead and we had taken seven POWs.

'I radioed the CO and gave him a completion report. He was thrilled. He asked me to name the boys who had died. I did. Then he asked about the wounded, so I told him the names. He immediately said, "Jayang, that's eleven—who is the twelfth man?"

'"It's me, sir." There was a pause. "I will see that the

wounded get evacuated, but we need a helipad. Jayang, how bad are you?"

"'I won't leave till I have finished my work here sir, and gotten all my boys back."

"Well done," and he signed off.

'By then my batman had got me a steaming bowl of thukpa. I had that and felt better. We collected our dead. It was a solemn occasion. They were all young men in their prime. We cremated them one by one. Eight pyres, just as the sun went up. Fourteenth of November 1971 was memorable—it was the day 22 Establishment had been raised in 1962, exactly nine years ago.

'The boys cleared the hill top and made a helipad so the wounded could be evacuated. We waited but from Delhi came orders that the wounded could not get picked up. The morale dipped. I could see it in the faces of the wounded. I called for my pack, distributed some dried raisins to each one and said, "We walk back, we will be okay." In my heart I understood that we, a Tibetan force, could not be openly acknowledged by India on the other side of the international border—no, not in the month of November 1971, when war had still not been declared.

'Sometimes things fall into place. One of the guides who had fled returned and led us back. By the time we reached the BSF camp in Lunglei we were exhausted. The BSF had made a barakhana for us. The CO was there, he greeted me with a hug. That night as we sat around the campfire, the CO, Colonel B.K. Narayan, said, "Long live the Dalai Lama, long live India-Tibet friendship. Jayang tum aur tumhare Tibeti sipahi sab sher hain"—all you Tibetan warriors are lions.

'The next day eleven helicopters came and ferried us away. The casualties and I were taken to the Silchar army hospital. I was there for eighteen days. When I was discharged, I reported to the transit camp and from there was airlifted to Rangamati where I met our IG Sahib and our leader Jampa Kalden. I was congratulated for the successful operation.

'When I returned to Sarsawa my CO gave me a paper saying it was my citation for an award.' Jayang picked up the file and, sure enough, nestled right on top was the paper, yellowed with age, typed on an old-fashioned manual typewriter. It read:

RECOMMENDED FOR GALLANTRY OR DISTINGUISHED SERVICE AWARDS

1. Number—51266
2. Rank—Coy/Leader
3. Name—JAYANG CHHERING
4. Unit—31 Company (Special Frontier Force)
5. Citation: -
    (a) Date/ Period covered by the citation—
        13/14/ Nov/71
    (b) Place of Action—JAILENPARI—Bangladesh
    (c) Qualifying Act—

This Company leader led the first assault on the extensively prepared defensive position of Jailenpari on 13/14/Nov/71. The enemy position was very strong with a platoon of Regulars, 150 MIZOs and 100 RAZAKARS. This company leader set an example of dashing courage by leading the first wave assault. He personally cut through the booby traps trip wire and he continued to do this and advanced through mine fields and heavy volume of fire from enemy defenses. He was profusely bleeding but he would not halt and continued to lead the assaulting wave and refused to be evacuated or fall back till after the capture of position. He showed courage and inspired his men to rise to a high act of valor.

RECOMMENDED FOR THE AWARD OF
CLASS ONE

Sd/ xxxxxxxxxxxxxxxxxxxxxxxxxxxxxxxxx
(BK NARAYAN)

Field   Lt Col
21 Dec '71   Commander South
                                      Column Force 222

Approved for Class One as Gallantry Award

Sd/ xxxxxxxxxxxxxxxxxxxxxxxxxxxxxxxxx
(S.S. UBAN)
Maj Gen
Force Commander

29 Jan '72   Special Frontier Force

Peering over his grandfather's shoulders, Tsering read it. 'Popo-la, did you get the bravery medal?'

Jayang smiled and shook his head, 'No, I got a cash award of 3500 rupees at the presentation parade held in February 1972. This is the picture. I was given the award by the IG Sahib.' Tsering stared at the picture of the tall Sikh officer shaking his grandfather's hand under a canopied parade stand.

The Medal

'But why didn't you get a medal, Popo-la?'

'Ours was a covert force and the operation we carried out was also covert. We can never be publicly recognized. But I got the biggest gift months later. After the formation of Bangladesh and the setting up of the Awami League government, we got an unexpected visitor—Sheikh Mujibur Rehman, the first Prime Minister of Independent Bangladesh. He had come to thank us personally. He asked for me and shook my hand and told me, "Jayang, the person who came to guide you all back to India was my brother. So I know of you."'

Jayang smiled at the young boy hanging on to his every word. 'That was my medal.'

In the Footsteps of Buddha's Warriors

OVER THE PAST year, ever since I started my collection of short stories on Tibetans, I have pored over books, researched manuscripts, and met a number of Tibetans. Of all the stories I heard and read, the ones that kept coming back to me were the unsung stories of the Tibetan resistance warriors. Trained by the CIA, they were the stuff legends are made of. Only memories and a few documents and photographs remain of that war—sepia-toned photos which show determined men with guns in their hands, radios strapped, a tungwa (lucky charm) and poison capsules tied around their necks. Traversing high altitude snowy passes into Tibet, these intrepid men had waged a guerrilla war against the Chinese PLA for fifteen hard-bitten years.

Many never came back. Those who returned faded into narrow alleys of Tibetan refugee settlements, unsung and unheard, their stories lying within them like a still, dark pool that hides all its pebbles.

The Tibetan armed resistance began in the 1950s when the Eastern regions of Kham and Amdo were overrun by advancing Chinese troops who bombed monasteries and subdued any opposition. That was when the Khampas came together to form the Chushi Gangdruk. Their singular aim was to protect Buddhism against the advancing Chinese. Gradually the Chushi Gangdruk, fighting the advancing Chinese PLA without fuss and fanfare, took on the mantle of 'Buddha's Warriors.' As Chushi Gangdruk's fame spread, more men from different regions of Tibet joined them. However, the Chinese forces were numerous and swarmed Tibet, forcing the Dalai Lama to flee to India in the month of March 1959. Buddha's Warriors were his human shield throughout that long journey.

The Chushi Gangdruk left the Dalai Lama at India's border and went back to Tibet to fight the Chinese. But they were hugely outnumbered, forcing them to follow in the footsteps of their leader and come to India.

India was turbulent. The new refugees were filled with bewilderment at a new world. Their collective anguish at the loss of their homeland far outweighed possibilities and hopes for their future. No one could think beyond their miserable present. Practically the only way to earn a living in India's mountain areas was to join road gangs building border roads.

The Chushi Gangdruk decided to resume their fight for their homeland.

It was in 1960, aided by the CIA, that they homed on to Mustang, the remotest part of Western Nepal. Till the eighteenth century, the 750 square miles of Mustang or the Kingdom of Lo as Tibetans called it, used to be a part of Tibet, until it became a vassal state of Nepal. It was ruled by a Tibetan king and had an indigenous

Tibetan population till as late as 2008 when Nepal became a republic. Jutting some 15,000 feet into Western Tibet, Mustang was too remote to be monitored by the Nepalese government. Its main approach from the south required a month-long trek from Kathmandu, through the Kali Gandaki, the deepest gorge in the world that lies between the two highest mountains, the Dhaulagiri (around 27,000 feet) in the west and Annapurna (around 26,000 feet) in the east. It was impassable from anywhere else. Mustang had many advantages as a clandestine guerrilla base.

From Mustang the Tibetan Volunteer Army repeatedly crossed into Tibet to collect information and create a spy network there as well as hit Chinese camps and convoys, sometimes meeting success, at other times losing their own. They were a constant irritant for the Chinese. The Chushi Gangdruk was the only resistance Tibet ever launched in its fight for their homeland—nameless, faceless young men who pledged their youth to die for freedom for their country. From 1960 to 1974 they continued this heroic struggle. Then in 1974 Mustang caved to internal and external pressures, ending fourteen years of Tibetan guerrilla warfare against the Chinese.

Forty-four years later as I avidly read accounts of the Chushi Gangdruk warriors, I was overwhelmed by the raw courage and moral fibre with which they fought, just two and a half thousand men, taking on the might of the People's Liberation Army, the largest army in the world. The more I thought about it, the more fascinated I was by the little-known narrative. Strangely, within the community there existed a shroud over the history of

Chushi Gangdruk. No one celebrated Tibet's only war for freedom. Save for books written by western and Tibetan writers as well as some Chushi Gangdruk warriors, the Tibetan community did not openly acknowledge their enormous history of bravery. It was as if this history was deliberately tucked away, layered under several folds of memory too deep and recessed to be feted. It left me puzzled and sparked my curiosity, because among mindful Buddhists who believe in karma this was a deliberate gap.

Among peace-loving Buddhists, the Chushi Gangdruk's fight for their homeland was the only fire I found. For a year I planned, failed, and planned again to get myself to Mustang. I wanted to see the wild countryside that had been the camping ground of these Buddha's Warriors. I wanted to map the ground they had walked, trace their footsteps and imagine what their epic journey and fight for the homeland must have been like.

Four decades is a long time, a whole generation gone by. Deep within me I hoped I would find someone who knew something about these unsung heroes, perhaps a Chushi Gangdruk warrior who had survived and carried still the flame of that distant forgotten war with the same passion with which he fought in his youth. It was foolhardy to expect anything so many years later but I was willing to take that ride, saturated as I was with history, the testimonies of some old warriors and bookish knowledge about the Tibetan Volunteer Army. I was ready to follow in the footsteps of Buddha's Warriors.

It was April of 2018—spring, the best time of the year to visit Nepal, resplendent with fragrant rice plantation, cool breezes and sudden showers. Crossing into Nepal from Siliguri, my husband and I drove to Pokhara. At Pokhara, unsure of the terrain, we hired a four-wheel drive with a driver. That is how we meet Dil Rai, the Scorpio driver, who belongs to Jomsom, the capital of my destination Mustang.

It is an eleven-hour backbreaking ride to Jomsom. Dil Rai sizes us up and nods. I have passed muster to undertake the journey which takes every ounce out of its travellers. We leave Pokhara while the early morning mist is playing hide-and-seek with its guardian deity, the Macha Puchere, allowing only the snowy top to peek at us.

Barely outside the city limits, we hit an undulating dirt road that was under construction. The construction efforts are focused on the edges where retaining walls and drains are being prepared. The middle of the road, where traffic traverses, is a quagmire of rock and potholes whose depth and treachery cannot be gauged. We are completely at the mercy of Dil Rai's maneuverings. He is skillful and his Scorpio eats up miles.

Each bridge we pass has a name, characteristic of the river or stream—names like 'Burbure Khola' or 'the Muttering Brook', and 'Bagane Khola' or 'the brook that carries you away'. A sign board catches my eye—'Modi Khola'.

'Ah, named after our Prime Minister.'

Dil Rai shakes his head. He is not a fan, and although he insists that he dislikes politics, I read the undertone of anger when he talks about India's economic blockade of Nepal in 2016.

'We were just recovering from a massive earthquake when India imposed a full blockade at the border. All because they wanted to impose their will in the making of Nepal's Constitution. Can any country interfere in the making of another country's Constitution? That is how it all started, and what happened? We were starved for food, petrol, cooking gas, all essential items and medicines. For everything we are dependent on India.' He shook his head, his eye on the road. 'But things will change. Sometimes adversity teaches you the biggest lesson. The blockade was a good thing, it showed us the way forward.'

'Which is?'

'Can't trust India. So we need an alternate friend.'

'China?'

He shrugs, 'Yes, we have to give them a chance at least.'

India is at an all-time low on popularity in Nepal. The latest popular rap song, a Nepali version of 'Despacito', is anti-India. It's a Catch-22 situation. On the streets, Indian cars rule the roost, with the most popular being the Maruti, despite almost 250 per cent import tax. Ready availability of spare parts helps, along with the formidable reputation Maruti has garnered over the years. The food and medicines are all Indian. Bhat Bhateni, the largest chain of malls, sells Chinese clothing and an array of shoes favoured by the young, but there is also a sari section which the women gravitate towards.

However, the past two years have seen an influx of Chinese tourists and Chinese aid touching every corner of Nepal—China is reconstructing many earthquake-damaged iconic buildings across Nepal. The hydro-dams are on their long to-do list. An all-weather road built by the Chinese links Nepal's capital city Katmandu to Shigatse, now known as Xigatze, a large prefecture level city, with an area of over 182,000 km, once the historical Tsang province now administered under the Tibetan Autonomous Region. A railroad is also being planned.

The road that we are travelling on will connect the Chinese border town to Nepal's Lo Manthang, the ancient capital of Mustang, to Pokhara, making Chinese access into Nepal multi-directional. All of this will change the geopolitical situation in the region. It's a dismal thought. The average Nepali like Dil Rai no longer thinks of India as a friend.

As the road climbs, Dil Rai points at the swing bridge that connects remote villages over the swift flowing grey Kali Gandaki river. Almost all rope bridges have been replaced by heavy duty steel girders, courtesy of China. I wonder what the Chinese influx will mean for the Tibetans in Nepal, and what it will mean for the Nepalese in the long run.

It's over three hours in the car, but the undulating dirt road is quickly forgotten in favour of the picturesque wild countryside. The traffic has dwindled to a mere trickle of jeeps and a few buses all headed to or coming from Muktinath, the shrine which is some two hours away from Jomsom at the height of 13,000 feet. It's a revered shrine for both Hindus and Buddhists.

The alpine forest is all around us. Ironically, the trackless dirt road we travel on and which the Chinese are building, is the same road that was once a forest trail through the Kali Gandaki gorge. The trail through which the Tibetan warriors undertook their journey to Jomsom, Mustang. I recall everything I had read…

It was after the spring of 1960 when the Tibetan fighters began arriving into Mustang. Young men who had been part of Chushi Gangdruk and volunteers collected from road gangs across India were organized into small groups in Darjeeling and Gangtok. In groups of initially just fifteen to forty odd men, they secretly crossed over from India into Nepal's dense jungles, walking westward. Using the forest cover, they camped and trekked through the Kali Gandaki gorge. It would be days later that they came upon the Tibetan plateau of Mustang— arid, windswept and cold.

The men were not told where they were going and why. If questioned by the border police they were to say they were on a pilgrimage to Chuming Gyatsa, housed in the compound of Muktinath. Buddhists believed that Guru Padmasambhava, the tantric seer responsible for spreading Buddhism across the Himalayan kingdoms, meditated here. That legacy still lives on and Chuming Gyatsa remains a sacred Buddhist pilgrimage site.

Each man travelling by road from Pokhara was given 165 rupees and a sturdy pair of boots with which they walked to Mustang. Soon about 2000 men had gathered in Mustang. More were on their way.

The wild jeep ride finally comes to a welcome halt. We stop for lunch at a tin-roofed shed named Hotel Muktinath where a noisy bus-load of Gujarati tourists are eating the local Nepali fare. I order the same and Dil Rai serves me; his relative runs the joint.

For hours we have been travelling the dirt track. From here the road is steeper as we climb, and then descend to climb again. The mountain road is precipitous—one wrong alignment of the wheel and the Kali Gandaki can claim us. Fields of maize frolic in the wind as if waving and cheering us on. The villages that line the road or are perched on remote hilltops are windswept. A few fields line the road, fenced off by grey stone walls. Something catches my eye—the surrounding massive rock faces have caves.

'Is this where people meditate?' We are skirting a village; stacks of firewood lie in massive bundles in the village square and laughing children run barefoot alongside the jeep. It's nearly dusk and a man is herding his cattle home.

Dil Rai stops and asks him if the caves are used for meditation.

The man peers at us, grins and replies in Nepali, 'No, it's where we keep the bones of our ancestors.'

We are silent as we move away. The caves are high on the sheer rock face and the only people for whom approach is possible are skilled rope climbers. People here follow an ancient culture of Bon Buddhism. The Buddhist prayer flags are everywhere.

We have been on the road for almost ten hours. The landscape is still alpine with swift mountain streams. For miles it's wild uninhabited countryside. Every turn brings in new sights of cedars, junipers and meadows of wild flowers. Nothing much has changed by way of geography. Mustang still remains untouched and remote but it stands poised on a threshold of change. The Chinese road will surely change everything, says Dil Rai.

We halt for tea in a tin-roofed barrack-like hotel. Polished copper pots are placed by the main door and hold brilliant red rhododendron flowers framed by deep green leaves. An excited dog barks its welcome. I sit on the verandah, taking in the panoramic view of the sweeping river valley. A woman brings us refreshing cinnamon-laced tea.

We are soon on our way. There is no road. Dil Rai banks steeply and eases into the sand banks of Kali Gandaki. I ask him to kill the engine for a while, as I sit awed at the enormous vastness that opens up in front of us. The dusk falls softly in orange, gold and magenta hues on a primitive and ancient land. We are sitting in the heart of Mustang. As far as the eye can see, there is not a single sign of habitation. We have left the tree line behind. Hills in shades of blue and purple rise, arid and treeless; the horizon is dominated by the Nilgiri and Dhaulagiri mountains, majestic and cloaked in glistening snow.

Dil Rai is quiet, letting me take it all in. 'Do you remember the Bollywood film *Khuda Gawah*? It had Amitabh Bachhan and Sridevi and was supposed to be set in Afghanistan.' I nod. 'It was shot here. The famous Buzkazi shot of the Afghani game of polo on horses chasing a dead sheep was shot in the open ground there.'

I recall reading how for centuries traders' caravans roamed the Kali Gandaki trail between China, Tibet and India carrying salt, yak wool, cereals, dried meat and spices. Dil Rai finally starts the engine and guns the jeep, racing along the sand banks. Surprisingly, the sand is rock solid and a relief from the undulating road.

Half an hour later the jeep climbs out of the sand banks and moves on to the road. The rutted track is lined with apple orchards framed by grey stone walls. The trees are resplendent with flowers and there is a sweet smell of the coming bounty that accompanies us. We are on the road to Marpa, Mustang's prosperous town. A little ahead past the apple orchards are rows of neat white houses with firewood stacked on the rooftops. They are all Thakali homes, Dil Rai tells me. The indigenous Thakali community is named after the Thak river. The Thakalis make up some 3 per cent of Nepal's population. For long years they were salt traders who later got into the hotel business. Thakali food is very popular with tourists.

We stop by the white gateway to Marpa and I walk down a cobbled street. It's delightful—spick and span with neat shops that offer colourful knitted woollens, herbs, joss sticks and Tibetan curios. A Buddhist monastery and temple stand at the heart of town. Up a steep flight of stairs sits the benign Buddha, and beyond on the rock face is a stupa styled gateway painted in the sitting image of the Buddha. It's striking, framed against a huge rock overlooking the whole valley. I am not sure if it leads to the abode of the dead, so don't hazard a guess.

Apple is the main crop of Marpa and the locals have fashioned it into delightful apple wine, and diced and sun-dried apple snacks. I buy a packet and find that the dried apples have retained their natural sweetness. Past the town, the narrow cemented canals irrigate fields of maize, wheat and apple orchards. Marpa is rich in natural abundance, an unexpected and delightful oasis in the middle of the wild countryside.

From Marpa, Jomsom is roughly half an hour away if you hit the sand banks. We race in the growing dusk as the grey waters of the Kali Gandaki catch the gold lights of the sun. All around the hills have turned deep purple and the snowy mountains are bathed in gold.

'Welcome to Jomsom' says the main gateway. It's cold and the wind has picked up. I pull on my jacket, smiling at the sign I pass for the Windy Valley hotel. My destination is Hotel Majesty. Dil Rai stops and carries my bag into the hotel. The hotel is a three-storeyed affair complete with a pool table, clean and efficiently run. My room on top has the Dhaulagiri peering at me. It is so close that the night cannot cloak its glistening snow peaks. In the soft moonlight I can see it resplendent and eternal. I sleep with the window shades drawn aside. Each time I open my eyes at night, I can't help smiling at the mountain under whose shadow I sleep.

It is under the same shadow of the Dhaulagiri that the men of the Tibetan Resistance Army slept once they arrived in Mustang. The mountain was witness to the groups huddled around camp fires, shivering and unprepared for the tribulations they would initially face. As more men arrived, beefing up their numbers to 4000, there was a severe shortage of food. Facing frostbite and near starvation, the men were forced to boil their boots to survive. Slowly the Tibetans began settling down to their new surroundings.

General Bawa Yeshi was appointed the leader of the new organization, now called Lo Drik-Tsang. He was appointed by Andrug Gompo Tashi, the man who started the Chushi Gangdruk resistance movement in 1958 in Lhokha, Tibet.

Gompo Tashi was aided in his resistance effort against the Chinese by Gyalo Thondup—the second eldest brother of the Dalai Lama. It was he who contacted the CIA to support the Tibetan cause. For the Americans, the Tibetan movement was part of their global anti-Communist campaign. They agreed to train the Khampas.

The Americans trained the Tibetans in guerrilla tactics, espionage, use of explosives, weapons, radio operations, map reading, using the compass and survival techniques. The first group of trained men were para-dropped into Tibet and were involved in protecting the Dalai Lama and ensuring his safe passage to India when he fled Tibet.

Meanwhile the men who reached Mustang christened it Zimbuthang because of the abundance of grass-like herbs. Their leader General Bawa Yeshi had been a monk in Kham and had received guerrilla training. Slowly he began organizing his men.

Help arrived in early January of 1961. Twelve men trained by the CIA in Camp Hale in Colorado, USA, were para-dropped and arrived in Mustang as a fresh breath of air in an atmosphere of starvation, frostbite, snow-blindness, death, and the dipping morale brought about by lack of food, resources and harsh living conditions. Their arrival boosted the men's flagging spirits. They chose 400 of the most physically fit men from all those who had gathered and began training them. The men were divided into camps, some in forward areas, others with yak hair nomad tents. All camps were located in hidden valleys while supply depots were closer to existing villages. In time there was a clear demarcation of troops—transport, supply, ammunition, intelligence and internal discipline.

Soon headquarters came up with buildings from where the Resistance Commander Bawa Yeshi operated. The flag of Tibet flew in the courtyard. Slowly an army-like discipline began to prevail.

The next air drop brought in more CIA-trained instructors, food and weapons. Gradually Mustang boasted of forty trained instructors from Camp Hale. They began imparting much needed guerilla training to the Tibetan warriors who learnt to operate American supplied Springfield rifles, explosives, heavy 80-millimeter recoilless guns, 2-inch mortars and machine gun silencers besides operating the radio, using solar-powered batteries and decoding messages. In addition to survival techniques, the men learnt how to use miniature cameras for spy work as well the use of death pills if they were ever captured.

Slowly the men adopted the khaki uniform and followed a regimented camp discipline: reveille, followed by basic physical training, singing of the Tibetan National Anthem, then training. By 1964, there were roughly 6000 men with arms in Mustang. There were basically two groups: one involved in infiltrating Tibet, and another in providing support, food, and clothing.

It was from these camps in Mustang that the Tibetan Resistance Army crossed over to Tibet and began laying ambushes on Chinese convoys operating on the Xingjiang-Lhasa highway. It was Tibet's main arterial highway that connected Kham, traversed the entire northern strip of the Himalayas onwards to the Aksai Chin region of Ladakh from where it travelled to Xinjiang and beyond to Soviet Union, covering 1500 miles of extremely sensitive border territory. This was the Chinese lifeline they were raiding.

For each raid a dozen men infiltrated into Tibet for a month, and the vast spy network they had been successful in running, with links throughout Tibet, helped them with information.

The raids were riddled with enormous difficulties. For centuries the Tibetans had used horses, but on these trips, they could not use their mounts as they were a dead giveaway. They had to trek all the way up to the raid sites and retreat in the same fashion after the ambush. The difficult part was always the retreat. Once the PLA learnt of the raid, they always sent fresh troops to cut off the Khampas' retreat. Jogging the whole night, putting in as much distance as they could, most guerillas died not from Chinese bullets, but from their bodies giving up. At such extreme altitudes, age catches up faster than the wind. The wounded were left to die as there were no medicines and no doctors to conduct surgery.

In one ambush they found a bag full of documents which was sent to the CIA for analysis. It was an eye-opener. For the first time Chinese official records showed that in the 1959 uprising some 87,000 Tibetans had been killed.

In October 1962, China unexpectedly attacked India. After the war ended, Tibetan men were asked to join a special force that India was creating. Many joined the Special Frontier Force called the 22 Establishment which was headquartered in Chakrata, Uttarakhand. Their one hope was that they would get a chance to fight the Chinese. For the first time, after the Chinese invasion of 1962, the Tibetan Resistance Army and the CIA had a new member—India. New Delhi became the headquarters of the joint operation run by America, India and the Tibetans.

Dawn arrives early in Mustang. The brilliant cloudless skies and glistening peaks nudge you awake. It is while having my breakfast that I meet Khagender, the owner of Hotel Majesty. He is a large Thakali man with a loud voice that brooks no argument. His family runs the hotel.

As we sit around having tea, I ask Khagender if he knows anything about the Chushi Gangdruk. He is on the verge of taking a sip when he stops, his eyes shuttered, his voice icy, 'Why? Who is asking?'

'It is for my book. I am writing on Tibetans. Jomsom was the Tibetan base, wasn't it?'

'I know nothing.'

'Aren't you a local?'

'Yes, but I know nothing, all the Tibetans are gone.' He turns away, stands up abruptly and begins shouting instructions to the waiter. I persist, 'Please Khagender Jyu, I am here for another two days, just in case there is some name, someone you remember…please let me know.' His behaviour leaves me surprised—a while ago he was a perfect host, and now he seems hostile.

Puzzled, I look out of the window. Dhaulagiri is resplendent, set against a glorious blue sky right in front of us. It's like being part of a postcard.

There is a faint drone which gets louder. A fixed-wing aircraft lands close by. The snows of Dhaulagiri had caught our complete attention and I had not even noticed the airport runway just across the road from our hotel. People are dragging suitcases or carrying rucksacks towards the plane. I can see passengers disembark with their cameras trained on Dhaulagiri. Khagender suddenly appears and says, 'The question you asked me a while ago...' I nod, waiting, 'I know someone who will be able to answer all your queries, but I will have to ask if he is willing to talk.' I hold my breath.

A short while later he returns, 'My brother, Nar Bahadur Hirachand, will talk to you. He has called you to the Gompa in Marpa where he will be staying for the whole day for the town prayers.' Brother is a loose term for a close acquaintance in Nepal. I nod, grinning. Finally, a light.

Dil Rai races me to Marpa. I had forgotten how riveting it is with its streaming willows, flowing canals and apple trees laden with blossoms. I climb the steep stairs of the Gompa, and the sound of prayer, drums, cymbals, and voices raised in prayers greet us. The cobbled courtyard of the Gompa has a huge flagstaff, an iron pole draped with the Buddhist prayer flag. Seated in a semi-circle with some other men is Nar Bahadur Hirachand, a thick-set man with a fleshy face and a Nepali dhaka topi. He is as curious about me as I am about him. He asks questions, watching me carefully all the time. The other men are also watchful, but silent. When he is satisfied, he nods and we are served tea. A monk comes and adds some brown powder to their tea—tsampa, or roasted barley flour.

Hirachand takes a sip of his tsampa-laced tea and says, 'I was eighteen years old when the first of the Tibetans began arriving in Lo. I spoke the Bhote language as I had Bhote friends. So I was used as an interpreter by the Tibetans. In 1959 a huge group of Dolpas, or wandering shepherds, came from Tibet with a massive herd of cattle.

They sold yaks for twenty-five rupees, sheep for just five rupees and horses for fifty rupees. They sold everything and went to India. A year later the Tibetan Khampas began arriving; initially we would see four to five, then more and soon there were over two thousand. They kept to themselves, but I know they had difficulty getting food, for I saw them burn yak fur and boil the skin for food.

'Then more men arrived and the Khampas started getting organized...there was money and food and they started setting up a camp. The Jomsom army camp now occupied by the Nepal army was originally set up by the Khampas. The training camps were hidden across the hills. Slowly, buildings came up. There were barracks, the Commander's house and office where they flew the Tibetan flag. A huge Tibetan mastiff was chained outside the office. It became like a garrison.

'I was contracted to bring them rations. I got their rice, pulses, oil, meat, vegetables, all through porters from Pokhara. They took the same route you came by. Initially, I was paid in dollars, then I started getting paid in bhatta, Indian rupees, and then Nepali rupees. Ferrying rations across was not easy as it took twelve days to a fortnight from Pokhara to reach Jomsom. Many a time I have carried boxes of dollars or bhattas for the Tibetans.

'Then the Khampas began building an airport—the same airport that is now used for civil flights for tourists. For days they laboured and one night I watched as they dug shallow trenches and set them ablaze making a sign that read 'Welcome.' A plane circled, parachuted some boxes and landed. I don't know who came on it. Later the Khampas made shirts with the strong parachute silk to ward off the wind. They were tall, strong-boned men. They made a striking lot. They were the kind who made you friend or foe forever.

'They were brave men, fighting for their country against one of the strongest countries in the world,' he says, after a pause. He himself was only a supplier and claims not to know much about the resistance movement, its epic battles and its unsung heroes.

'We would see them training and we could hear the firing. I know nothing of how they fought against the Chinese. They were expert horsemen; they learn to ride as children. But they could not use their horses against the Chinese as they would have given them away. So I understand that escaping from raids was the most difficult part of their raids. In Zimbuthang there was that palpable excitement of men at war. I have met Bawa Yeshi, he was a man with mesmerizing speech. He loved to wear different clothes, sometimes he would wear a chuba, sometimes even a daura sural like a Nepali. But it was General Gyato Wangdu, the man who replaced Bawa Yeshi, who had great vision. He spoke English and had western education; he was years younger than Bawa Yeshi but he was a leader of men.'

He pauses again, frowning, then adds, 'I know one old man who may tell you more. He is not well these days and is hard of hearing. His name is Wangyal. He was a Khampa fighter—one of the few left. He used to be a manager at the Hotel Annapurna, close to the airport in Pokhara. It was the hotel that the Tibetan resistance bought as a safe haven for them. It was an asset for employment of old resistance warriors who could not fight anymore. If you can find Wangyal and if he talks, you are lucky.'

He plies me with food and more tea and as we talk, I ask him why he and Khagender were so suspicious of me when I asked about the Tibetans. He looks incredulous, 'You are educated, you can figure that out. The Chinese are everywhere—they are coming into Nepal in a big way. The people who are most afraid of their influence are the Tibetans. We have had their salt and we can't let our friends down. So anyone asking about them is screened well.'

I return from Marpa with Hirachand's words ringing in my ears. I am determined to find Wangyal. But first we drive around Jomsom and go slowly past the army base which used to be the Khampa headquarters. It's humming with activity, full of new buildings and barracks with no trace of anything Tibetan. In the compound, the battalion flag flutters along with the Nepalese flag.

My only Tibetan link is a name—Wangyal.

It's three days later that Dil Rai grins as he drops me off at my hotel in Pokhara. After quiescent Mustang's wilderness, Pokhara is noisy. It is a city in a hurry. That is why old people like Wangyal ferret themselves away and are difficult to trace. 'Hope you find your Bhote Baje,' Dil Rai says as he leaves. I smile since he has equated Wangyal to my Tibetan grandpa. 'I will,' I say, more confidently than I feel.

The next day in a local taxi I go up and down the airport road asking for Hotel Annapurna that had been taken over by the Gandaki hospital. No one knows it, so we end up outside the Gandaki hospital.

Past serpentine queues I reach the Registrar. Luckily, he knows about Hotel Annapurna. His directions are specific; he tells me to look for the crossing of Nagthaan or the snake altar and then turn right. I do just that.

In the relative quiet of the side road lies a double-storeyed old-fashioned hotel with a driveway and a beautifully laid out garden. The painted sign on the gate says Gandaki Medical College. The hotel is now a hostel for nursing staff of Gandaki hospital. The watchman directs me to a grey building that appears to be the staff quarters. It is where Mr Wangyal lives. I stand at the bottom of the deserted looking building, calling out to him.

A woman peers from the first floor. Her face is shuttered as she inquires who I am and what my business is. When I explain that I have just come from Mustang, giving Hirachand's reference, she purses her lips saying Mr Wangyal is sick and does not entertain visitors. I gently ask to meet him just for a while as I have come all the way from Dehradun, India. She finally calls me upstairs and makes me sit in the verandah. She brings me some lemon tea but she is nervous and hostile. She looks at the gate to see if I have come with someone. When she sees no one, she sits watching me, telling her beads.

I wait. Mr Wangyal walks in. He is a tall man in his mid-eighties with piercing eyes and the erect bearing of a soldier. It is obvious he is not well. His hands have liver spots and there are a few smatterings on his face. However, he still belongs to the dwindling breed of old-fashioned gentlemen who show courtesy to visitors. He hears me out patiently, then tells me that he is sick and knows very little about the Khampa army. His wife hovers close by and insists it's his lunch time. Their reluctance to speak to me is obvious so I make a last-ditch effort and ask if I can come back again around 4 p.m. once he has rested. He agrees.

When I come back, he is waiting for me. The atmosphere is warmer and he starts with, 'It's alright, ask your questions. I don't have very long to live... one year, at the most two.' He is not looking for pity, just stating facts. He allows me to use my notebook as he starts talking. His words are simple, yet the images he evokes are powerful.

'It was way back in 1948 when I was an eighteen-year-old monk that I joined the Chushi Gangdruk in Lithang. The Chinese had come into Lithang in 1949 and by 1958 they were mercilessly killing people. They bombed and vandalized monasteries. During the clash, two of my brothers died. My land and my people were enough motivation for me to join the Chushi Gangdruk.

'Gampo Tashi and Gyato Wangdu made an army camp and taught us the basic do's and don'ts for fighting the Chinese. We had heard of the involvement of Gyalo Thondup, the second-oldest brother of the Dalai Lama who had contacted the CIA and sent men to be trained in America. It felt good to know that such a powerful nation was helping our cause. We would fight during the night, lying in wait for the Chinese and then attack them. Lots of Chinese and Tibetans died in our fights, but we didn't have time to count our losses. Very soon everywhere we went in Tibet the Chinese were already there. We heard that the Chinese were trying to capture the Dalai Lama from Norbulingka. So we were divided into two groups, one group under Andrug Gompo Tashi were to protect the Dalai Lama, while the other group would wait by the riverside and ward off any attack.

'In Chumdogyang a fierce fight with the Chinese took place. The Chinese threw bombs and some of our fighters were killed but the Dalai Lama reached India safely. By then more Chinese troops had come in and we realized we were outnumbered and had to stop fighting. We reached Montawang—the Tibetan name for Tawang, Arunachal Pradesh—in India, by the end of March 1959.

'After a few weeks of living in the camp we wanted to return to Tibet to fight again but we had surrendered our weapons to the Indian troops and were not allowed to go back. We were sent to Missamari where, at the age of twenty-five, I went to a school and was taught basic Hindi and English. A year later I was sent to Kalimpong, a small hill station in Darjeeling district of West Bengal. I was among the men who didn't want to do road construction but wanted to return to Tibet to fight for my country. That is how we came in contact with Andrug Gompo Tashi again.'

He takes a sip of warm water from his glass, encouraging me to pick up my lemon tea. 'There is an old Tibetan saying, "No point in worrying if you can't do anything and no need to worry if you can do something."' He smiles but it never reaches his eyes. I can imagine him young, with nowhere to go, a refugee whose only way back home was to fight for it. Hauntingly similar to the epic tales of Shenpa, the brave hero of Ling Gesar whose tales of bravery passed down from generation to generation orally until the eleventh century when they were written down. This epic is in 120 volumes of a million verses and is twenty-five times the length of any western classic. Besides being the longest epic in the world, it is considered the greatest work of Tibetan literature. Immensely popular among Khampas, it is often the reason why they become warriors.

'That was the time the idea of Mustang as our base began to become a reality. I left India and entered Nepal through Butwal, then to Pokhara and onwards to Jomsom, Mustang. There were others like me. We found ourselves in complete wilderness. At a distance I could see deer and antelopes, there was no habitation. We had nothing to eat, we quickly lost weight. We washed and boiled our leather boots to survive. There were about 2,400 men and it was bitterly cold at night so we would cut juniper and cypress branches and cover ourselves with them. Even now at times when I sleep, I can still remember their fresh smell. It has never left me.'

He takes another sip and a comfortable silence lies between us. I let him travel the distant path etched so well in his memory.

'Months passed, then the men Andrug Gompo Tashi and Gyalo Thondup had sent to the US for training came back. They began giving us guerrilla training. We were divided into thirteen groups and each group was further divided into two for administrative purposes. Everyone's aim was the same—fighting the Chinese. The CIA air-dropped weapons and materials inside Tibet which we had to go and retrieve. Yet another time they dropped weapons in Mustang. We felt brave with our weapons.

'In 1962, when China attacked India, a friend and I were sent to Pokhara and we set up a shop from where we sent rice, food and clothes to Mustang. I went to Kanpur and bought boots for the men, bought khaki cloth and got a tailor to stitch uniforms. In 1964 we rented a restaurant and it was here we got supplies sent by our people that came in by air to Biratnagar and Kathmandu. The restaurant was the collection and distribution point. From here in Pokhara we ferried all the things to Mustang using the Sherpas...' he pauses.

'Around this time, from what I have read, the camp had issues with corruption?' I query. He nods, not saying anything. For proud Tibetans like Wangyal to talk of what went wrong is often painful and mortifying among strangers like me. I let him talk and tell the story the way he saw it, nodding and making notes, registering his silence and sometimes smiling as he looks over his shoulder, groping for the right word from his wife. We speak in Nepali. Outside in the stillness of the approaching dusk, rain falls softly and it gets dark.

He is tiring and I can see that as we part. He stands up to say goodbye, and enveloping my hand in a warm grasp, he wishes me luck. His eyes tell me we will never meet again.

His words and my research are a perfect match, filling gaps in the narrative.

What he left unsaid is the tragic story of how in the

mid-1960s Gyalo Thondup acted on a long-standing complaint of corruption against the Mustang commander Bawa Yeshi, who had embezzled funds sent by the CIA. Bawa Yeshi was recalled to Dharamshala and offered a job. General Gyato Wangdu, nephew of late Andrug Gompo Tashi and the sole survivor of the first group of Tibetans trained by the CIA, was appointed the Commander of Mustang.

Bawa Yeshi refused the job offer at Dharamshala and a month later returned to Mustang to create a breakaway group of two hundred men. It was the start of internal fault lines in the Tibetan guerrilla movement.

Strung far away from the mainland, the Tibetan warriors were unaware that the world around them was changing and a new world was being created that would collapse their cause forever. In the 1970s a series of events took place that jeopardized the Tibetan resistance movement. President Nixon became US President and he sent his closest aide to China to find a solution for ending the Cold War through US-China reconciliation. The very first demand of Mao Tse-tung was that the Americans had to stop all help to the Tibetans. The Americans informed Gyalo Thondup that they were pulling out, but would aid the resettlement of the Tibetan warriors in Nepal. Their other partner, India, had built up the Special Frontier Force made up completely of Tibetans since 1962. It had grown into a mature force and had even fought on the Indian side during the 1971 Indo-Pakistan war. But, like America, India too was now looking at ways to improve ties with China.

For the Tibetan leaders it was devastating news. They decided not to inform their men but to continue as long as they could under General Gyato Wangdu. They also began to work out a plan for the resettlement and employment of the warriors.

The Tibetans purchased land and built Hotel Annapurna. More land was bought, a carpet factory and handicraft centre were set up in Pokhara and Kathmandu, a transport service between Pokhara and Kathmandu was also set up—all aimed at providing employment and creating assets that would generate income for the warriors in their time of need.

The Chinese meanwhile began exerting huge pressure on the Nepalese King Birender to evict the Tibetan resistance from Mustang. In 1973 the Nepalese publicly asked the Tibetans to disband their camps and surrender in exchange for rehabilitation, aid and land.

When the Tibetans did not surrender, Nepal tapped on to the internecine rivalry. They forced Bawa Yeshi to present himself to the capital where he was interrogated by none other than Nepal's Home Minister for almost three months. Slowly they broke him down. Finally, pleading for protection and political asylum, he gave detailed accounts of the Khampas' strength, weaponry and positions.

Armed with inside information, in 1974 the Nepal government asked the Khampas to lay down their arms. They even sent an emissary to General Wangdu to ask him to surrender, offering him half a million dollars plus all the property and buildings the Tibetans had constructed in Nepal. But General Wangdu wanted to fight and so did his men. A bitter and bloody standoff was in the offing.

Afraid that a bloodbath would ensue, very unexpectedly the Tibetan government representative and personal emissary of the Dalai Lama, Phuntsok Tashi Takla, arrived with a taped message from His Holiness asking the resistance to lay down their arms. As the tape was played across all resistance camps, pandemonium broke out. Many wept, overwhelmed by the situation, and some highly respected Tibetan leaders like Panchen even slit their throats. More leaders committed suicide as the message of laying down arms by the Dalai Lama spread. For the proud men who had sacrificed everything with the single aim of fighting for their homeland, this was the biggest surrender. They could never go against their God King's words and yet they had pledged never to surrender to the Chinese. Surrendering to Nepal meant the same. They now had nothing to live for.

The resistance began surrendering and the Nepalese troops began disarming and arresting them. Nepal went back on their word as mass imprisonment of Tibetan resistance leaders began and general amnesty was not granted to them.

When General Wangdu heard of the arrests, he fled to Tibet with some forty men and important documents. But the PLA was lying in wait. He was forced back into Nepal only to be ambushed by Nepalese troops. During the firefight, one of the mules carrying food was lost. General Wangdu sent two men to get it back. While one man returned, the other, who belonged to Bawa Yeshi's camp, fled down to Jomsom and reported General Wangdu's escape route to the Nepalese troops.

The Nepalese army using Bawa Yeshi's men set out on General Wangdu's trail. Another faction guided the Nepalese troops to set up an ambush point some 20 miles from the Indian border at the 17,800-foot Tinker Pass in Jumla district.

It was here that the battle-weary General Wangdu and his men reached and dismounted, unknowingly in sight of the ambush party. Seeing his tired men, General Wangdu with a party of five, went to look for water and some food. The moment the six men came down the pass, a storm of gunfire erupted and rider-less horses came galloping back. The men raced to see their leader General Wangdu gunned down as he charged the Nepalese position. A fierce firefight ensued and many from the resistance were killed. Finally, seeing they were outnumbered, the remaining Khampas scaled the neighbouring heights into India.

A day after the firefight at Tinker, Bawa Yeshi was flown in a helicopter to identify General Wangdu's body. Following the confirmation, a ceremony was organized in the Royal Palace where the soldiers who had taken part in the Mustang operations were awarded by the King. In Kathmandu's Thundikhel grounds, in the middle of the city under a large tent on display to the curious, milling public were General Wangdu's rifle, tea mug, amulet, wristwatch and rings—the last remains of the guerrilla leader. An assortment of arms and ammunition from the Mustang Tibetan camp was also on display.

With General Gyato Wangdu's death, some twenty-five years since the Chinese invasion of their homeland, the fight for Tibet was tragically over.

It was to a hostile world that the men of Chushi Gangdruk returned. The hands that once wielded guns had to learn new skills—knotting carpets, driving taxis, rearing chicken and pigs or setting up small shops selling artefacts—dying a little inside each day as they let go of the warrior in them. By 1974 when they returned, they realized they had been waging a remote war in a remote corner, too clandestine to touch the collective conscience of an indifferent world. In the fourteen years that they had been fighting the war, the Tibetan movement had taken the path of non-violence and dialogue. The path more difficult, as the world had crowned their God King an apostle for peace. In such a world there was no place for violence and war. The more the world embraced Buddhism, the more the Tibetan community closed ranks to ferret away in its recesses the heroic war fought by the Chushi Gangdruk, ensuring that it remained unsung and unfeted.

Soon the sands of time took over. Young strapping warriors, now leaderless and still torn in two camps, one that Bawa Yeshi created, and the bulk who remained faithful and proud of their fallen leader General Gyato Wangdu, slowly turned into old gnarled men. Years of living on the battlefield had broken their bodies and left them with limping walks and weak eyesight. Fading into narrow warrens they lived isolated, quiet lives. Their heroism and sacrifice went ignored by the community. Many feared their stories would die with them—this only promoted a sadness and a new hardness that hinged on resentment, a wistfulness for acceptance from the community.

The wait was long.

For a community that took all its cues from the Dalai Lama and the Kashag, the first public acceptance of the freedom fighters came almost eighteen years later in December of 1992. They were received in Dharamshala on the occasion of 'Tenshug' or long-life ceremony for the Dalai Lama. The security office of the Tibetan Government in Exile issued to them certificates that had their names, serial numbers, date and place of birth, along with the father's names. Inscribed on the certificate was the statement that the person had joined the Chushi Gangdruk organization of his own free will from 1960 to 1974 and served the country with full dedication.

It was the first official confirmation of their courage, dedication and love for Tibet. For the old men in the winter of their lives, this ultimate acceptance was all they had craved. They had enough time to remember their days as warriors. Months would pass without them thinking or talking of Mustang, then someone would ignite the fire and wonder what would have happened had the CIA and America continued to fund, train and equip them—would they have achieved Rangzen? That was an answer they could never come to. Some felt America had let them down while others felt that as Buddhists it was all a part of their karma.

Unknown to them, the Americans too had the Tibetans on their mind. Their CIA operatives who trained the Tibetans had fallen in love with the simple rugged men whose love for Tibet made them constantly take leaps of faith. Internally, there must have been debates and lobbying for the Tibetan cause. As it was all clandestine, no one will know what undercurrents transpired. But in September of 2010, an unexpected celebratory ceremony took place in the mountains of Central Colorado. The US Forest Service unveiled a plaque to commemorate the training by the CIA of Tibetan freedom fighters at Camp Hale, Colorado. The event included the former CIA agents and Tibetans involved in the operations along with some family members, and was the first public validation of their history.

A plaque erected there read:

'From 1958 to 1964, Camp Hale played an important role as a training site for Tibetan Freedom Fighters. Trained by the CIA, many of these men lost their lives in the struggle for freedom. They were the best and the bravest of their generation and we wept together when they were killed alongside their countrymen.

This plaque is dedicated to their memory.'

GREEN
Water

Kutta Ama

'Nagri, Sho-sho, Mari sho-sho la. Sho-sho.'

A flurry of black and golden-red mongrels race through the sun-dappled triangle of Dehra's Shahanshahi Ashram, Old Rajpur and Jharipani towards a mango tree, responding to the cries of an old chuba-clad woman. Her eyes light up, she counts them loudly in delight as they rub against her, jumping and licking her hands. 'Sho Sho,' she welcomes them as she lays down their bowls of shredded buns and milk. There are too many to count now, so she calls them by the colour of their fur in Tibetan. The blacks are Nagri and the golden-red are Mari, which does not do full justice to them since it means red. The dogs don't mind; they understand instinctively that she loves them.

Everyone calls her Kutta Ama, the mother of dogs. Years of hardship have etched their marks on her once fair skin, and her white greasy hair is bunched and held back with rubber bands. She is dressed in a dark chuba and fleece jacket to ward off the winter cold. Her pangde, the long apron with geometrical lines, is tied over the jacket. Twenty summers since her husband's death, she still wears it in his memory. Her feet are shod in worn keds come winter or summer as she walks long distances to reach her dogs. But it is her eyes that draw you to her. They crinkle up and overflow with warmth as she reaches to pat a dog, her calloused hands gentle while crooning in soft broken Tibetan as they lie down on their backs, exposing their stomachs to her in complete surrender.

Every afternoon, unfailingly, whether in the bitter winter cold, lashing rains or blistering heat, she takes a bus all the way to the tri-junction where her dogs await. Carrying an old oil-stained shopping bag on busy Rajpur road, she is invisible to the world. Walking through a warren of narrow lanes with crumbling desolate old havelis, she stops at a tiny shop that sells milk and knick-knacks.

Smiling broadly, the shopkeeper calls out as soon as he sees Kutta Ama trudging in. 'Amala, Tashi delek.'

She answers him sitting on the small wooden stool at the entrance of his shop. It's where he perches himself in his free time, watching the multi-storeyed building that is coming up on the adjacent plot. In his lifetime, he constantly grumbles, the landscape of Rajpur is changing so rapidly, and new-fangled cafes with English names like Marigold and Rivoli are mushrooming so that soon he would lose his way back home.

He was a young boy when Rajpur had suddenly come alive with an influx of Tibetan refugees. They were a silent, brooding lot who kept to themselves in cliques, smiling and bowing with folded hands in greeting as they spoke no Hindi then. Slowly and unobtrusively they built their monastery close to the Sai Mandir and colonies around Rajpur. They merged, learnt Hindi and Indian ways and were accepted as a peace-loving community who wore a distinctive dress and had a language and culture that was soon identifiable. The colourful prayer flags that initially flew around their colonies and temples gradually got copied by modern Indian cafes, found swathed on rooftops and even hung in car windows or motorbike handles of the young as good luck charms.

'Dhiru Bhai, did you see a black puppy someone had left on the road yesterday?' she asked, as the old man bustled around in his small box-like shop.

'Oho, Amala, no. Come to think of it, how many dogs can you afford to feed?' She smiled, ignoring him, scouring the bushes with her eyes. 'Must have been a kuttiya. No one wants one. She will litter every season and fill the roadside with puppies.'

He picked out five packets of sweet buns. Each packet contained two buns and two packets of milk that she would need to drizzle on them.

She reached inside her chuba and took out her small string bag, counted the money and gave it to him.

His cell phone rang and he picked it up, 'Haan, kya bol raha hai?' he frowned, then stopped Kutta Ama from leaving.

'Amala, wait, Langrah wants to talk to you.' Langrah was an aged cripple who walked with crutches and often sat with Amala under the mango tree, regaling her with tales of the five mongrels he called his children.

She looked up from the stool puzzled, 'Me?'

No one ever called her. And why did Langrah want to speak to her?

He held the phone out and she took it awkwardly, 'Hellooo?'

'Amala, Amala, please Amala, I have no one to ask this, I can only ask you. Can you please look after my dogs while I am in hospital?'

She heard the pleading and thought he was crying. 'Hospital? Why are you in the hospital?'

'I fell off the bus. The driver drove away while I was getting off. It's a miracle another bus didn't run me over. I will live, Amala. This time I have fractured the thigh bone. Can't put weight on it and it's in a cast. It's my children I worry about.'

'Of course I will look after the children, you look after yourself. Don't worry.'

'I'll pay you back Amala, I promise.' She dismissed this and handed back the phone.

Langrah lived in the cowshed of Dhiru Bhai. He had an indifferent son who lived in Dehra town with his pinch-faced wife and two children. At the start of every month he would come to pay the rent and reluctantly leave his crippled father some money to survive. He disapproved of the dog squad his father surrounded himself with. But Langrah had once told Amala that he missed his family and the dogs filled the void.

She stood up and asked for another packet of milk and more buns before leaving the tiny shop, walking steadily through the meandering street towards the tri-junction where her dogs stay. She called out to her dogs and found two of them missing.

She called out again, her voice rising and falling as she walked to the ashram where some old dogs would find a quiet place and sun themselves, but today they were not there. She sat a while with misgivings. Slowly she walked to the huge municipal dustbin, still calling for them, but the monkeys were busy rampaging. They really were very badly off since their forests were taken over by people. Trees were cut down and lantana bushes, home to hundreds of bulbuls and sparrows, burnt to make way for multi-storeyed buildings. Their forests merged with ever expanding city limits. So now the monkeys lived as beggars in the very land where they had once lived free and with aplenty.

There were too many monkeys and too little food. Dehra was growing without design or thought, abandoning its meadows, litchi orchards, canals and ivy-clad tin-roofed bungalows—discarding everything that once made the town distinct and genteel—all in a hurry to become the perfect clone of a smart city. The monkeys too had learnt to be in a hurry, and so those who made it inside the dustbin impatiently rummaged and threw out plastic bags with stale, leftover food after they had eaten their share, dumping it in an untidy heap. This attracted the hungry dogs who ate what they got, and after they too were done, rambling bulls ate what they could from the rotting filth.

The monkeys could jump off the dustbins and take off to the trees when they sensed danger. The loitering dogs were not so lucky. They were easy targets of young men with too much testosterone to let off, who would take bets on who could crush the dogs. Amala had seen young boys speeding on motorcycles ram deliberately against unsuspecting dogs. Their cries of triumph would be louder than the whimpers of the dying dog.

Amala hated such boys. As a lifelong Buddhist it had shocked her initially to feel such enormous anger boil inside her and make her so blind with hate that she picked up a rock in outrage and hate. The first time one boy astride a scooter had deliberately run over a small puppy, she had picked up its broken body as it screamed in agony, unmindful of the blood drenching her chuba, crying in pain for the little pup. She had nothing to offer to it except her presence.

'Saala janwar,' the tea shop owner had spat in anger, picking up rocks to hurl at the monstrous boys. They had fled, jeering. The shopkeeper had got a shovel and helped Amala dig a small grave by the roadside.

Today the shopkeeper heard her calling for her dogs and told her that he had seen one old black dog limping towards the Jharipani road. 'It couldn't have gone far as it was walking with great difficulty.'

Amala nodded. She had been getting some Tibetan medicines for the dog's arthritis and mixing it with his food. She walked slowly. A kilometre down the road by a culvert she found him. His inert body was stiff in death. He had come down seeking a lonely spot to die alone.

She walked back and asked for the shovel. The shopkeeper looked up from his gas stove and called out for Chotu to help Amala. When she returned it was well past seven and the tea shop was closing.

'Amala, have some tea,' but she shook her head and walked on. She still had Langrah's dogs to feed.

She took a long while to return to the Tibetan Old Age Home, a nondescript white double-storeyed building that was just off the main Rajpur road. It was well past nine at night and dinner was long over. Bhole, the chowkidar, a cantankerous old Bihari man who doubled up as gardener, was angry at being disturbed. He had a small transistor next to the fire he had lit for himself, preparing to stay warm in the long winter night that stretched ahead.

Amala invariably missed her dinner. Today was no different. While the gate was to close at 9 p.m. every night, Bhole had begun closing it at seven.

When Amala called out, 'Bhole Bhai, gate kholo,' he yelled at her from the fireside. 'You cannot come in, it's way past nine today and I can't open the gates for a mad wandering woman. Mad woman. Mad woman,' he muttered, repeating himself loudly.

Any other day she would have argued, cajoled or bribed him with tea money, but today she sat wearily by the cemented curb, too cold and worn out from the day's happenings. Langrah's dogs had whimpered in bewilderment as she fed them and ensured that they stayed the night in their cowshed home. With the old dog dying, she felt as though someone close to her had passed. She didn't care if Bhole never opened the door.

'Amala, Amala, are you alright?' Bone-weary, she had leant against the wall, closed her eyes and fallen asleep. Bhole stood over her, his eyes wide, then squinting to see if she was alright.

'Amala did you have an accident? Shall I wake up the Superintendent Sahib?' She shook her head as he helped her up.

They climbed the ramp two floors up to reach her

cold sunless room and she thanked him. 'Stay well Amala, whom will I fight with otherwise?' She smiled and waved him away.

She washed her hands in a small bowl and took off her keds, too worn-out to cook herself the bowl of instant noodles that would usually be her dinner, then lay down, letting sleep claim her.

To the eighty odd inmates of the old age home she was Sangay Choezam, the woman crazy for dogs. Kutta Ama was the name given by the people of Old Rajpur. Her connection with dogs was karmic. She never knew her date of birth but she was sure she must have been born in the year of the wood dog, whichever year that was. While people travelling down roads take in new sights, Amala looked out for dogs. The more unwanted they were, the more she sought them, feeding and talking to them. Unlike other inmates she did not tell her beads as she walked the roads—instead she was a one-woman salvation army for strays.

Surprisingly, money came unexpectedly to her, without her even asking for it. The Tibetan doctor gave her medicines for the dogs and also money for their food. Some shopkeepers gave her money on birthdays and death anniversaries. The biggest amount she received was from the Dehradun Municipal Corporation. They gave her eleven thousand rupees in cash besides a mounted certificate in her name for the work she did with stray dogs. She never spent any of it on herself. She ate in the Old Age Home; the only exception was the instant noodles she bought and kept for dinner.

When she had returned with her certificate, the Superintendent had smiled and said, 'Amala, now even Maneka Gandhi knows of you.' She didn't know who that was. When she looked nonplussed, he added, 'Indira Gandhi's son's wife and a minister now.' Amala nodded, Indira Gandhi she knew. Her father Jawaharlal Nehru had been the Prime Minister when the Tibetans had come to India.

She had been a wide-eyed ten-year-old then, holding hands with her elder sister, as they joined the Tibetan exodus in 1959 from Kongpo in U'tsang to India. Their father looked after the farm of the noble family of Yuthok and felt duty-bound to stay back, along with their mother and brother, sending the girls to safety with their uncle. After over fifteen days of walking treacherous mountains they landed up in Dibrugarh in Assam, frightened, famished and afraid of being turned back home.

From there they came to Tezu and joined a Tibetan settlement which was a large farm. Amala and her sister became a part of the labour force—transplanting rice, weeding fields of maize and vegetables and cutting the harvest.

The hard labour and the heat sapped them of energy and left them prone to illnesses. Two years after reaching Tezu, her sister succumbed to the raging fever that swept their camp. Amala survived, but with her sister gone she felt truly alone. The farm became her life. Years passed. It was a hot summer day when she was about twenty-two that she noticed a small itchy patch on her hand. Despite the medicines, the patch—wet, sticky and purple—spread in size every day. Soon it began to ooze and smell foul.

Her uncle said that she had probably developed the problem which as per Tibetan belief stemmed from touching Lu or something dirty. When no amount of Tibetan medicine worked, she took to wrapping her hand in a handkerchief and had to stop working. That was when her uncle sent her to Dharamshala to the Nagpa who would treat her through his tantric powers.

Three months into the Nagpa's treatment the wound receded and finally disappeared. To sustain herself she began working for a restaurant, washing dishes, waiting tables and helping out in the kitchen. She was thirty when her uncle got her to meet Karma—an enterprising man five years younger than her, who had built a carpet factory through sheer hard work. The two married and Amala began helping him in his work. Their business started booming with orders that poured in from Ladakh. It was a good life.

Then Tashi, Karma's younger brother who lived with them and was a fun-loving lad, fell in love with an Indian girl. To their dismay the girl got pregnant and her outraged family came and created a huge fuss. To add to their woes Tashi disappeared. Every day the girl's family came looking for Tashi, their anger simmering to the point of violence. The night the girl's brother beat up Karma and broke a loom in frustration, Karma said, 'I will sell this place, we must leave. It can't go on like this every day, they will burn the factory down.' She agreed to his decision.

Overnight Karma sold his factory. They took a bus to reach Kulu, joining a Tibetan settlement where most people were employed in road building. In the dusty roadside under a tarpaulin she gave birth to a little girl. They named her Drechen. It wasn't much of a life after owning a factory. After almost three years they took a bus and reached Clement Town where Karma was asked by Kochen Rinpoche to look after a carpet factory. Even Amala picked up a job in the tiny settlement, monitoring the water supply to their colony.

A year later Amala gave birth to their second child, a son. But years of subsisting on very little nutrition affected the child who was born weak. He didn't survive long, dying just before his first birthday, leaving her heartbroken. When she recovered from the blow she concentrated on their daughter, proud to watch her study and do well in school. Slowly they rebuilt their lives, living in a small hired flat.

With the festival of Losar approaching, Karma was working full time to get some orders completed. One Sunday he returned late, climbed up the stairs to their tiny flat and complained of heaviness in his chest. It felt as if a huge rock was weighing him down. The doctor said he had respiratory problems caused by constantly having to work with wool. 'Your blood pressure is also erratic so you will have to take medicines every day to keep it steady.' Karma nodded. He had a big order to complete. Careless about his health, he rarely remembered to have his medicine. A day before Losar the air of festivity was everywhere and Amala was busy cooking when Karma's assistant ran to call her. Karma had collapsed at work, suffering a massive attack.

By then their daughter Drechen was married and had

two children of her own. She stayed a few houses away and ran a small ready-made clothes store. Drechen had always been a wilful child and they had indulged her. When she decided to marry the boy of her choice they had complied with her wishes. But after her father's death, Drechen was of little solace to her widowed mother. Amala wondered if this was because she had been too busy at the factory and that had made her daughter feel neglected and hence resentful. She had asked her once but Drechen dismissed the conversation.

Not wanting to be dependent on her daughter, Sangay began selling bags of candies, chips and chewing gum to children going to school. It barely fetched her any returns so when she saw that it would not sustain her, she walked to the Tibetan Settlement Office and asked to be registered in an Old Age Home.

Her daughter didn't come to see her as she packed up her flat. Amala despaired at the growing indifference with which her daughter treated her. When she went to say goodbye, she was shocked to see that her daughter's house was locked as was the shop. A neighbour told her she was out of town to get a consignment of clothes for her shop. Sangay nodded, climbing the mini bus that had come to fetch her. Four large bags stuffed with personal belongings were the only things she carried into her new life. The Old Age Home was now her forever home.

Adjusting with others in the home and listening to their stories only depressed her. She began sitting on the sidewalk of the bustling Rajpur road near a popular institute that offered multiple management courses, watching the young students flood the street with chatter and enthusiasm. Just sitting on the sidewalk, she vacillated between past and present easily. She often thought of an old woman she had met in her time in Dharamshala while she had walked her kora.

The kora is the daily perambulation that devout Tibetans make, walking around the periphery of a monastery. Amala had often seen an old woman with a broom sweeping the kora—she would be there wearing a makeshift poncho cut from a large plastic sheet, unmindful of the rain, the winter cold or the summer heat. One day when she was resting, Amala walked up to her and asked if she could sit with her. The old woman patted the cemented culvert invitingly.

'I see you sweep the kora every day. How long does it take?' Amala asked.

'The whole day, so I start around ten and by five I am done. During the rains it takes longer,' she smiled.

'Why do you do it? Has anyone asked you to?'

The old woman shrugged, 'No one has asked me. When you reach my age, you understand that there are always two choices for everyone in life. I had a choice of sitting in the compound of the old age home, taking up a useless quarrel with someone, yelling and passing the day. It's so easy to do that. I thought long and hard about how I can make myself useful. One day while walking the kora I saw the wind had carried plastic bags and rubbish, littering parts of the kora. So the next day I came prepared with this broom. Now I stay busy, while I sweep I say my prayers and I am useful to others.'

Amala had sat there mesmerized by the old woman's words. Despite her gnarled knobby hands and the dirt under her nails, she had a beatific smile and a native logic that stayed with Amala for a long while. She realized that sweeping was the old woman's salvation.

On a busy Friday evening Amala saw a small black furry pup walking along with its siblings, following their mother. But while others crossed, he stood disoriented in the middle of the milling traffic. Amala, unmindful of the traffic, picked up the little pup. When she took him to safety and set him down, he tried following her and stumbled, hitting himself against the curb. That's the time she realized he was born blind. She knew that alone he had no chance of survival. So she put him in her shopping bag and smuggled him past Bhole to her room.

Crooning softly to him, she let him curl up next to her in bed. It felt wonderful to have the warmth of the little pup. He trusted her and followed her around the tiny room. She laughed, playing 'scent-me-out' with him. For the first time after Karma's death Amala felt happy. She looked forward to spending her time with the little pup. Every day she would feed him milk, spreading old newspapers across the room before she went for her morning prayers. When she returned after her morning meal, she would clean up the mess, put him inside her big canvas shopping bag, cover it with a shawl and leave. She would walk to the meadows nearby and set the pup free. He would run small distances, playing happily with a ball she had bought for him. She felt the sun and fresh air were good for him. In her mind she called them their little picnics.

The first time she climbed the bus with Chotu in her bag and went to the Shahanshahi Ashram, it was like an excursion. That was when she began noticing other homeless dogs scavenging for food. She got buns and milk and fed them. It became her regular outing with Chotu. When she got off the bus with Chotu the dogs ran to her, welcoming her as if they were meeting her after years. It was the most heartening part of their excursion; besides, Chotu got to make friends.

When Chotu was tired they would return. She didn't feel lonely any more. 'What should we name you, little one?' she asked, as he slept trustingly on her lap. She laughed as he made suckling noises and snuggled closer. She held him close, kissing his cold wet nose, and even in his sleep he wagged his tiny tail.

'Chotu,' she said running her hand over his sleeping form.

Chotu was her shadow and the love of her life.

It was Bhole who stumbled upon her carrying Chotu up to her room. At five months, he now filled the shopping bag and hated to be carried in it. What was worse was that it was difficult to haul him up and down the ramp as he was heavy. Bhole's eyes became round orbs when he saw Chotu.

'Amala, you know the rules about keeping pets here?' She nodded, her heart thudding in fear. The Old Age Home sprang into action. The Superintendent, a genial man, looked shocked. Amala was told it was either Chotu or her.

'He is blind, he will never survive without me, please,

I beg you, let me keep him. I promise he will not litter or do anything bad.' She felt the same fear that she had on seeing Karma's still body. She couldn't dream of a life without him. She would die without him now and she was sure he would never survive without her.

'Amala, the Home has rules. We look after you but we cannot take your pets too. You can give this pup to an animal shelter. If you want, I can arrange it.'

With tears coursing down her face, Amala set Chotu by the main gate of the Home. She had nowhere to take him. And she did not want to give him to an animal shelter where there were so many dogs to be looked after—who would take special care of a blind dog?

Chotu wandered around while she sat down by the cemented curb and kept watch. After some time when he had tired of sniffing and playing around, he came and curled up next to her. The winter sun dipped and a cold breeze blew in from Mussoorie. Amala put him on her lap and wrapped a shawl around herself. Chotu curled up and fell asleep.

When the dinner bell rang, although Amala was forced to go for her meal, she barely managed to eat. Her heart was heavy. She had set Chotu down by the gate wrapped in her shawl. It would give her an excuse to go back.

When she returned, the Superintendent was there with Bhole. They had closed the gate and Chotu was outside. He had come out of the warm folds of the shawls and was whimpering for her. 'Bhole will keep watch, Amala, you please go to your room. It is for the best.'

Kutta Ama

Reluctantly Amala went up, tears falling from her eyes for a long while she paced her small room. She could hear Chotu's whimpering and it broke her heart. Not too far a furious dog fight had erupted. It galvanized her into action. What if the street dogs tore up Chotu, her helpless blind pup? Carrying another shawl to ward off the winter chill she crept down the ramp. It was quieter now and she saw Bhole starting a small fire. She opened the gate and Chotu was curled up on her shawl. He was shivering as the wind had picked up and was piercingly cold. She picked him up, wrapped the shawl around them both and sat on the curb, closing her eyes.

The Superintendent on his late-night rounds saw Amala sitting hunched up against the wind, the pup in her lap. He sighed. Bhole looked at him and said, 'How long does she have to live sir? Only some years. Without the pup, half of that.' The Superintendent said nothing and walked away.

Dawn was breaking and the birds were chirping in the tall sal trees when she woke up. She opened her eyes to see Bhole and the Superintendent looking at her worriedly. She started guiltily and Chotu peered from under the shawl, his little nose sniffing.

'You will get sick being out in the cold like this, Amala.'

She looked down at Chotu. 'He is all I have,' she said, caressing the little pup tenderly.

The Superintendent said softly, 'Amala, I have a solution.' She looked up, her eyes shining with hope, waiting, 'I think the old quarters of the Old Age home behind the kora are not being used, so you can keep your pup there but not in your room.' Amala's eyes filled with tears.

Then, carrying her Chotu, she shuffled along with Bhole and the Superintendent towards Chotu's new quarters, mumbling, 'Bless you, bless, you, bless you.'

The Three Nightingales

Snow God of Song
Lend us your song key
If we get the key we will be great singers
On this beautiful earth
We have invited fairies to shower good fortune on all beings

TRANSLATED INTO ENGLISH, the ancient Tibetan way of how minstrels start their singing loses much of its native flavour, but this is how Dolma, Yangchen and Nawang start every musical session at marriages, festivals and auspicious welcomes. In the Tibetan world they are among the last remaining traditional women singers of their homeland, affectionately nicknamed the Three Nightingales.

Now in their seventies, their voices have matured and mellowed and when they sing the sonorous high notes it sounds like the wind sweeping the plateau and raising a storm that fills the soul of every Tibetan. You can feel the grit in your eyes, you can smell the mud matted with yak dung and you can hear the laughter of the gurgling cold rivers as they frolic by. The songs make the past and present one.

At one special wedding the three singers looked around

the room rife with excitement as the bride's long hair was braided into the customary plaits. The young radiant girl sat on a stool with a large mirror, surrounded by married women who tittered, combing and braiding, counting the number of plaits loudly. Small talk and teasing laughter gamely accompanied the innuendoes.

Dolma remembered her mother saying 108 is a good number when she was getting married herself. 'Why Amala?' she had asked, and her mother had smiled, still holding her hair, 'That's what my own Amala said when I was getting married.' But she told her later that 108 represented the number of volumes of the Tibetan book of Kun Djur. Her mother began singing and they sang together, tears rolling down their cheeks. It would be the last time they would be doing that before she was married and her life changed forever.

Her mother's songs had brought them close together, as close as peas in a pod. But it wasn't always like that. Too much had happened in her childhood that kept them apart. She could still recall the rancid metallic taste of fear when their family had walked, sore in the feet and dizzy with hunger, following a multitude of panic-stricken people fleeing Tibet in 1959. The night stop was where she had first encountered her friends, Yangchen and Nawang, both strangers, who too appeared to be seven years old, and who mirrored her bewildered face.

She was the only one who had managed to travel with a battered wooden doll that her father had fashioned for her from smooth wood. It wore scraps of her old chuba. Her mother had laughed as she painted on eyes, nose and black lips using burnt twigs from their hearth. It was all smudged up now and at first glance appeared faceless. Nevertheless, in the cold mountain stoop where families stopped for the night, she held out her doll to the other two and they became friends. Their faces lit up as they twirled it around and laughed at its ungainly, droll appearance.

'What's her name?' Nawang asked.

'Pema-la.'

The girls giggled aloud, cupping their mouths, 'As if she is a princess.'

Dolma grinned back.

Dolma, Yangchen and Nawang all belonged to small hamlets in U'Tsang. As they continued up the mountain pass, from time to time they held hands, pulling each other along, cold, hungry and frightened, urged on by parents carrying infants and the few household treasures they could salvage. Only Nawang's grandmother was on a yak; the others had to leave their grandparents behind. As the mountain became steeper, people were leaving a trail of treasures behind—swords, boxes, utensils and clothes. From far away the scattered clothes looked like sleeping people who had been left behind in the snow. The treacherous slopes made the girls closer, the journey etched like a scar in their memories.

When they reached India, they stayed together in a camp run by the Indian civil authorities. The heat of the plains was unbearable. They had never seen so many trees growing so close together as they were used to sweeping, rugged, treeless open spaces of their homeland. India was suffocating. They discarded their woollen, leather and fur-lined clothes and boots, and wore the cotton clothes provided at the camp. Everyone moved around in a daze. No one understood what the dark-skinned people said or the strange food they ate.

Soon, their parents had no choice but to begin working as labour on border roads, creating destinations where none existed, cutting through forests and mountains like pioneers. Only, none of the new destinations ever headed home. Their mothers too worked while the children sat by dirt heaps, playing in piles of broken stones. The girls minded their younger siblings as best as they could. At night, they cooked on makeshift hearths, burning the firewood they collected, eating their hastily made meals, and sleeping under tarpaulins on the hard earth. Days blurred into months and they learnt a smattering of Hindi. They learnt they were in a place called Kulu and their parents were making the highway to Leh. Everyone felt this hard life was temporary, and soon the Dalai Lama would lead them back.

But many years went by. The girls became inseparable. When Dolma turned eleven, her family decided to migrate to Dharamshala where their relatives had settled down. She begged her parents to leave her with her friends. They were the only anchors she had, as the parents worked from sunrise to sundown. But Dolma's parents were adamant. On the day Dolma was to leave she hugged her two friends tight, imprinting their smell and warmth in her heart. 'Don't ever forget me,' she said sobbing, as she climbed the lone bus that was to take the family to Dharamshala. Tears blurred her eyes when she watched her friends running after the bus, waving and calling to her till the bus turned a corner and she could see them no more.

~

Dharamshala was bustling. Dolma had never seen such a huge settlement of Tibetans anywhere. She was by then strong and raw-boned, looking older than her eleven years. Her rosy cheeks had faded to dusty sunburnt brown and her hair had grown long, reaching in a raven cascade below her hips. The little brother and sister she minded were now old enough to be left on their own. She began to work alongside her parents, building the temple of His Holiness and other landmark buildings of the Tibetan Government in Exile. She never went to school although there was a big drive to get Tibetan children educated. Her siblings went instead.

With her working, the family was much more comfortable. The Losar festival they celebrated when she turned sixteen was memorable. For the first time in years her mother got them new clothes to wear and there was an air of festivity as relatives came home and celebrated with them. It was there that she first heard her mother sing old folk songs. She was struck by the sheer beauty of the songs and the pictures they painted. Her mother's voice rose like the gentle caress of the wind on the highlands and meadows, the tinkling sound of waters and the soft smoke from the Ba.

'I never knew you sang so beautifully Amala, you never sang like this ever,' Dolma told her mother once the guests left. Her mother's soft pink cheeks had lost all their bloom in India's dust and the ravages of her labour had left their mark, turning the smooth skin to its wrinkled, aged shadow. But the songs she sang changed her to the young woman that still lived within her.

'When you have to eke out a living, songs don't come, my daughter.' She pulled Dolma down to sit next to her and combed out her long hair, braiding it into a plait.

'Will you teach me too?'

Her mother nodded, her heart swelling with pride. She sang, asking Dolma to follow the lines with a wistful smile. Dolma did not know how to write down the songs, and so she learnt them by heart and they wrote themselves out in her memory as she sang. Every day she and her mother set some time together after their work. Dolma loved to sing. She had a lovely voice. She learnt that there were songs for every occasion. There were harvest songs, drinking songs, marriage songs, love songs and even songs for the Lhu, sweeping sonorous ballads sung by the nomads.

Singing opened up the doors of memory for her mother. One day, Dolma found her sitting by the kitchen hearth singing snatches of a song she remembered.

'What are you singing, Amala?'

'I am trying to remember the song I heard as a child sung by Khampa minstrels who travelled from village to village singing about a wild, impulsive Khampa boy who conquered the kingdom of Ling.' She frowned. 'I am afraid it's a long song and I have forgotten what I heard as a child only a few times when they came to sing in our village.'

'The song, what was it about?'

'The song is an epic of King Gesar who had supernatural

powers. He could be present in several places at the same time. He could, out of nothing, create ghost caravans, complete with horses, tents, lamas and hundreds of horses. During war, he could create an army of supernatural warriors who would kill the enemy and subjugate demons from all four corners of the world.'

Dolma loved the story and she learnt the few snatches her mother remembered. Singing changed the environment of their home. It was as if there was a bubbling happiness all around.

She was seventeen when she married and her mother sang the marriage song, tears streaming down her cheeks as her friends braided her long hair and helped her into her wedding finery. Dolma cried for the family she was leaving behind. She left her home carrying the songs her mother taught her as her legacy.

In her husband's home, during the ceremonies where his family welcomed her with khatags and gifts, she looked up and was jolted to see a woman her age whose smile was hauntingly familiar.

As the woman's arm rose in greeting with the khatag, she asked softly, 'Nawang?' The woman stopped and looked at Dolma closely, sweeping her into her arms with a cry of recognition. After all those years, the two friends had found each other. Nawang's parents too had moved to McLeod and had married her to Dolma's groom's cousin, Pema. The two friends lived close by and were a great comfort to each other. They often spoke about Yangchen, the missing third in their trio, and wondered where she was.

Dolma taught Nawang her songs and they would sing and laugh together, crooning the songs to their children as they became mothers. They felt lucky that they had each other and husbands who were also friends and family. The children grew up becoming fast friends. When they grew older, they were schooled in the Tibetan children's school as boarders, leaving the mothers with the time to help their husbands earn and also look after the elderly in the family.

Dolma's husband, Nordup, ran a small shop of trinkets and beads on the road leading to His Holiness's temple. Nawang's husband, Pema, had a sweater business and would travel out of town often during winters to sell these.

Dolma had three strapping sons and yearned for daughters. She assuaged her love for a girl child by becoming a godmother to Nawang's two daughters. The children grew up quickly and each time they came home they looked taller and more mature. They poked fun at their mothers whom they felt were still steeped in the old ways. Their world had opened up to new things, new ideas, computers and the internet. Life was changing for the Tibetan community.

It was on a summer break when their firstborns were sixteen that the two mothers had gone to the market. Laden with purchases, the two women were walking through the main square of McLeod Ganj when they saw a young man engulfed in flames running through the market screaming, 'Free Tibet, long live the precious Protector of Tibet!' For a moment nobody moved, unsure of what was happening. The two women stopped in their tracks, fear clutching their throats, as the young man collapsed in a flaming heap close to them. Someone ran over with a blanket which he threw over the flaming apparition, trying to douse the flames. More people ran carrying blankets as the smell of burnt hair and charred flesh filled the air.

A crowd gathered. A hush fell. The bustling market was completely silent. Some young men tore through the crowd, lifted the charred lifeless body on to a charpoy and ran towards the hospital.

Within minutes there was a huge crowd as word of the self-immolation spread. Dolma and Nawang were astounded to see their children there as well.

'Why are you here?'

'The boy who self-immolated was from my class and a good friend of mine,' Dolma looked at her eldest-born and felt weak with fear.

Nawang's daughter was there too and many of the classmates clung together crying. Pandemonium ensued and shops closed down as the marketplace swelled with a sea of people. Till now the two mothers had heard of self-immolation in Tibet, of monks dousing themselves with kerosene, offering their bodies as light in the darkness of Chinese-occupied Tibet. They had read of how Tibetans had found the most non-violent way of protest, and read about each death with increasing sadness.

'With today's self-immolation, the figure is now 150 people who have died for Tibet. Our young brother is a martyr,' said a young man with intense eyes and a red bandana. The two women recognized him as a poet and writer of repute.

Dolma and Nawang found themselves buffeted by the crowd; they left their purchases in the shop closest to where they had been standing. The serpentine crowd moved like one wave towards the boy's home. Once they reached the crowded flats, they watched the boy's distraught mother crying, holding her daughter. It was Yangchen.

Ironic that they had found their friend in that terrible moment. They learnt that Yangchen was a widow, with no extended family to rely on. Seamlessly the two friends began taking care of Yangchen and her family. They became her anchor.

~

Tipa road falls on the Bhaksu road that leads to an ancient temple of Lord Shiva, also called Bhaksu Nath, worshipped by a vast Hindu population across Himachal Pradesh. But the entire McLeod Ganj, named after Sir Donald McLeod, once Lieutenant Governor of Punjab, is largely Tibetan since the Dalai Lama came and set up residence here. Rows of houses stand precariously, built on steep stoops as flats. Sharp steps lead to a small flat where Dolma lives. Nawang's home is adjacent, and on the opposite side of the road is where Yangchen has her flat. She moved there when her daughter married, so that she could live close to her friends.

The three friends have, much to their sorrow, outlived their husbands. Once their children grew up, they took a deliberate decision to live close by. Their friendship has kept them going. Beyond their circle, the world around them has been changing so rapidly that it often leaves them as bewildered and unsure as the time they had first stepped out from Tibet into India.

They are grandmothers many times over but the young people's life is a puzzle. They are constantly busy and their grandchildren's children even busier. This is a constant lament for the three friends. After school, they return to tuitions and once home are on their cell phones or computers. No one badgers their grandmother with tales of what they did that day or insists on stories at night. Instead they lock themselves in their rooms, insisting on privacy. Their frenetic lives, always so hooked and animated, make the old women feel like unwanted fossils.

For company they do have each other. Most days they sit in each other's homes, settled on comfortable settees that double up as beds at night. Their feet are ensconced in hand-knitted socks and shawls wrapped around their chubas to ward off the cold. Years of hard labour have taken a toll on aging bones. All of them have arthritis that leaves them with an unsteady gait and painful joints. Their prayer beads never leave their hands, wrapped like beaded bangles around their wrists. They sit, sipping warm butter tea and often watching a video that a nephew has made of them singing. They laugh as the video starts, gamely pulling each other's legs, remembering the wedding where they had sung, dressed in brocaded chubas, standing as good-will ambassadors.

Singing was how Dolma and Nawang got Yangchen to start life afresh. It was Dolma's idea to be an all-ladies singing group. She spoke to all the women in their prayer group. They baulked—it was alright to sing among friends and families but in front of unknown people who could laugh at them, it was intimidating. But Dolma was a motivator. She insisted that they were the keepers of tradition and had to pass it on. The only way they could do that was by singing and reminding the people of traditional songs that had been sung for thousands of years in Tibet. But her friends were still afraid of being laughed at in their old age.

Dolma had snorted when she first heard their fears, 'What's better—to be laughed at, or for these songs to be forgotten?' So the group came together. At first they met in Dolma's tiny home but it was always too crammed. Later they took walks and sang in the open, with the trees and the slate grey Dhauladhar mountains as their silent audience. Sometimes curious passersby stopped to listen to the songs that sounded like the winds sweeping through a meadow of swaying ripe barley.

The first time they were invited to sing a welcome song for the Dalai Lama, at the start of the yearly function of the Central Tibetan Administration, Dolma could not believe her ears and her friends were shell-shocked. No one slept the night before. They tittered nervously that they were being teenagers once again. They practiced till they were hoarse and too exhausted to continue.

They had never been in His Holiness's presence. They had only joined the crowds that lined the two sides of the road holding khatags and lighted incense, as he drove past in a black Mercedes, his hand raised in blessing and a smile lighting his benign face.

On the day of the big event they wore their best chubas

and stood in the hall, their heads bowed, as the Dalai Lama walked in and took his seat at the head of the celebrations.

The eleven women singers stood and waited for Dolma to start. The traditional song of welcome with its clear notes rose in the silent hall, painting pictures of their ancient homeland—haunting, moving and lilting, merging the past and present as one.

~

Everyone told them they had to pass on their songs to the younger generation. They came back buoyed and determined to do just that. Only they found no takers.

They asked their children but they were always too busy, running homes and rushing to work.

'Singing? Amala, I have no time to breathe,' Dikye, Dolma's daughter looked up in mock horror. She was always rushing to meet deadlines, send the children to school, rush to office, rush back home. The rush was an endless cycle.

Dolma had retired hurt. Her friends too spoke of how they had been ignored by their children and of their reluctance to learn the old songs.

Things will change one day, they believed; so they let this pass, singing at weddings as that was the only occasion when everyone wanted to be steeped in their tradition. They did it all for free but if a family insisted they stay on for the wedding feast and pressed some money on them, they took it gladly, dividing it equally and calling it their 'tip.'

Dolma could hear age making its presence felt in their

voices. They devised means for each one taking on high notes, laughing at each other when their voices cracked. 'We are all getting old. Old traditional songs are only left to the old.'

'Have you heard the new Tibetan songs? They are always saying I-love-you,' Nawang said in disgust. 'How can you say that all the time? But they are selling really well and raking in money and fan followings.'

Yangchen laughed aloud, 'And we are always giving blessings. Who wants blessings in front of I-love-you? If I was fifty years younger, not me.' They laughed but they all knew it was the bitter truth.

There was no place for their kind of music anymore. They were just its marginalized guardians who had been banished to the remotest corner of young Tibetan conscience.

It was a divide the Nightingales knew they could never bridge. Then their oldest singer Dechen fell ill. She was nearing her eightieth birthday but she died a month short. The next year they lost three more members. Slowly their numbers were dwindling and no one volunteered to replace them. The three friends would attend all the funerals and walk home wondering who would be next.

'Looks like we are the three oldest trees left standing,' Dolma said as they sat in her tiny flat, drinking tea while a bone-chilling wind blew outside. They had still found no young people who wanted to learn their songs. But one good thing had happened. Nawang's nephew had written down their songs and made a song book. To have a song book they could pass on to the next generation made them feel good.

They turned each page although they could not read, smelt the book and smiled up to Nawang's nephew as he stood there grinning, 'This is all very well but what if the young never pick it up?'

He shrugged, 'Maybe they will never sing like you do, but who knows...maybe they could pick up the songs to sing and tune them differently like a remix version.'

They all laughed, 'It may sound like the I-love-you songs.'

He laughed alongside and said softly, 'But if that happens you may find your peace—the past and the present will then surely merge as one.'

YELLOW
Earth

Tibet with My Eyes Closed

I see Tibet's clear blue skies,
Her towering snow-capped peaks
Her verdant hills and valleys
But only with my eyes closed.

I see my dear homeland,
I see the home where I was born,
I see all my childhood friends,
But only with my eyes closed.

I'm returning to Free Tibet,
I'm back in my old hometown,
I'm re-united with my family—
But only in my dreams.

Why is it that,
It is only in my dreams
And only with my eyes closed
That I can see Tibet?

And why is it that
The good things in my life
Happen to me
Only in my dreams?

*Will I wake up one morning
To find myself in Tibet
And really, truly find
That I am not dreaming...*

*Yes, will I ever return
To an independent Tibet
And will I see
Tibet with my eyes?*

LHASANG TSERING LOOKS up. How many poems like this he has written, he wonders, and how many more will he write? He has taken to distributing them as bookmarks so people can read them. Not too many read these days.

He sighs. He was born in the year of the Water Dragon. That was the year 1952, exactly 900 years after the Tibetan saint and poet Milarepa walked the earth in 1052. The poet saint is revered in Tibet for the over 100,000 songs he wrote. They have been translated in English in a book called the *Shambhala*. Milarepa's songs and poems have influenced Lhasang greatly.

He stands up and stretches. He is a thin wiry man, with sundried skin, and a white straggly beard that grows like that of a billy goat in the middle of his stubborn chin. His eyes are electric. He does not mince words, so he finds he has little company he can tolerate or who can tolerate him.

Everything he knew about Tibet, Lhasang had soaked up from his parents. His mother told him that they were on a pilgrimage to India and had already passed through Bodh Gaya and Sanchi when his father, a devout Buddhist, had a premonition of his own impending death that coincided with a national disaster. He died on that pilgrimage while their homeland was torn asunder by the Chinese occupation. Braving all odds, his mother along with her two sons camped by the lake side of Rewalsar, north of Mandi, performing the forty-nine-day death rituals. Then the first of the Tibetan refugees started coming into India in 1959, and the family learnt they would not be able to go home ever.

For sheer survival his mother was forced to start working as a labourer in a road building gang in Kulu. It was from this dusty roadside that smelt of tar and smouldering cinders that Lhasang and his brother were picked up and put in school. They were among the first fifty students from roadside labour camps who were brought to Dharamshala, and from there sent to Mussoorie to form the nucleus of the first Tibetan Children's School in India.

To assist the Tibetans, American missionaries came in to test their IQ. Bright and immensely curious, Lhasang walked in for his tests with trepidation that the white people had come to convert them to Christianity. His brother deliberately failed the test, advising Lhasang to do the same. But once in the room Lhasang's innate curiosity got the better of him and he passed. He was sent to Wynberg Allen School, Mussoorie. Books became his passion and the library his haunt. The boarding school opened up his world, but also took him far from his Tibetan roots.

He was fifteen and buried into his ninth Reader's Digest when he read and re-read a story titled 'Raids into Tibet'. It was a fascinating story of how Tibetan guerrilla warriors based in Mustang, Nepal, were carrying out raids into

Tibet. One raid fetched them documents that showed how many Tibetans had perished since the Chinese occupation. The story ignited his pride and passion in being Tibetan.

That night as he lay in bed, he recalled every word. The story was etched in his mind and he was determined to become a guerrilla warrior and fight for Tibet's freedom. He knew however, that he must not voice this ambition, as everyone would dissuade him from such adventurousness. On the world map he located Tibet and Nepal but could not figure out where Mustang was.

Around this time his class teacher tasked them to write an assignment—'My Ambition'. He sat with the paper a long while, wondering how to keep his real ambition hidden and answer with something acceptable instead. He homed in on the much-coveted profession of doctor, and wrote that he would serve the Tibetans suffering from a host of health issues if given the opportunity.

Like all Tibetan children his essay was shared with his sponsors—a rich American family who owned almost half of Orange County. He was offered a medical seat when he finished school. But when he refused the medical seat the sponsor was paying for, he was hauled all the way to an audience with His Holiness.

He grins at the memory, 'Even before I could complete my three prostrations, His Holiness was on his feet. 'Why did you say no to becoming a doctor when we need doctors in free Tibet?'

Brought up in a western school, he hadn't realized the decorum of addressing his God King, and his words tumbled out, 'But we must have a free country first. Let me fight for my country. Free it. Bless me, give me a talisman and let me go.'

His Holiness stopped in his tracks, his eyes crinkling up with laughter, 'The boy is right.'

The Dalai Lama gave him a talisman and he was sent to the Tibetan Government in Exile's security department. He waited impatiently for his journey as a revolutionary to begin. He read up extensively about the American guns, the plastic explosives, the pistols, soaking up everything he could lay his hands on about Tibet. He was raring to go. Every day he would start his morning by running uphill, almost eight miles of a heart-pumping route, followed by push-ups and lugging cans of water for his mother.

He met some old Chushi Gangdruk fighters, too senior and battle-scarred to be of any use to a fighting unit. With no money and no means of earning a living, they lived together on the generosity of relatives. They were a quiet lot, men who had dedicated their lives to fight for Tibet's freedom, shutting their hearts and minds to the company of women and thoughts of setting up a family. They leaned on each other; their filial bonds stronger than bloodlines. Like ancient trees, they waited for their leaves to fall.

Lhasang would spend most of his evenings with them, listening to their memories of life as warriors of the faith. When they talked of Mustang, their eyes lit up with inner fires. And did they have stories to tell. Those who survived the Chinese onslaught had retreated with their commander, General Gompo Tashi.

Once in India they moved secretly, making their way from Darjeeling into thick alpine forests in small groups of forty to fifty men through the Kali Gandaki gorge into Nepal's arid, windswept plateau of Mustang. Mustang had been taken by Nepal as a vassal state in the early nineteenth century and stood as a wedge at 15,000 feet into Western Tibet.

They spoke with reverence of General Baba Yeshi, and General Gyato Wangdu Mustang Commanders, and their eyes crinkled with laughter as they recalled their camp days... of flying Tibet's flag, singing their national anthem and their life in remote mountain camps. These stories reminded Lhasang of tales about the American Wild West. One old man spoke of the CIA paradropping some forty graduates into Changthang along with a huge cache of arms and ammunition. This party who walked into Mustang as instructors and fighters were to streamline training and battle drills. It was from them that the men learnt how to use the Springfield rifles, the heavy 80-millimetre recoilless guns and 2-inch mortars as well as the solar batteries that ran radio hook-ups. They were all given the death pill to wear around their necks.

Lhasang clung to their words. Mustang's greatest strategic advantage was its proximity to the Xinjiang-Lhasa road that originated from Kham and ran along the northern scrap of the Himalayas. It was one of the two main arteries that started in Kham, meandered 1,500 miles onwards to the Aksai Chin region of Ladakh, moving on to Xinjiang and the Soviet Union frontiers. It was this highway and camps of the PLA that the Tibetan warriors attacked, ambushing convoys and retreating, the local Tibetan population, their mainstay in spying and providing shelter. The wild isolated countryside helped in such guerrilla wars.

The old men recounted hardships of having to leave wounded comrades behind, as their camps lacked medicines and doctors. Most wounded ended up taking the death pill or shooting themselves. The retreats after the attacks were the worst, fraught with danger and difficulty. Each time they returned to camp, some of their comrades were not with them. No one spoke too much of those left behind as each man knew it was the fate he had signed up for. It was a tough life, but that they fought for their country kept their morale high.

At night the tales of these men transformed and took on a life of their own, blurring reality and dreams. Lhasang's scrapbook was full of sketches of strapping Mustang warriors in their chubas, fur caps and guns, framed by harsh jagged mountains. He did not have the physique of the Mustang warriors but he had a stout determined heart with only one aim—a free Tibet—the land where his ancestors had walked free and where their bones had found final resting grounds.

While his friends moved on to higher education Lhasang stayed back, determined to become a revolutionary who would ensure the return of all Tibetan refugees to their homeland.

It was in early 1972 that Lhasang reached Mustang. The arid mountainside was everything he had dreamt of. With his sharp intellect he could quickly grasp ground situations. He estimated that there were some sixteen camps spread across the Mustang region, along with supply routes and intelligence bases that housed some 2,500 guerrilla fighters—to take on the might of the largest army in the world.

Their small numbers did not deter the Mustang warriors. They had pledged their lives to free their homeland and how strong and how heavily armed the Chinese were did not matter. They had soaked in the guerrilla training and there was just that much information sharing among them as was necessary. In case they were caught and tortured, they couldn't give information they knew nothing about.

Lhasang trained in small arms and information gathering and was dying to see action when, unknown to him, his world was all set to be changed forever. He kept a diary, writing down everything he did.

The Americans and the Chinese mended fences and Nixon went on a state visit to China. The renewed ties were to have long-term effects on the Tibetan resistance fighters. The first diplomatic concession made by the Americans at the behest of the Chinese, was to stop aid to the Tibetan guerrillas in Mustang, Nepal. Once that happened, Mao Tse-tung pressured the King of Nepal to flush out the Tibetan warriors.

Lhasang and like-minded young Tibetans appealed for the Tibetan administration to declare Mustang as Free Tibet, since already the upper reaches beyond Jomsom were completely Tibetan. Lhasang came down to Dharamshala as an emissary to beg the Dalai Lama not to give in to international pressure. But the Tibetan government gave in. Many Tibetans felt that perhaps Indira Gandhi had pressured the Tibetan government to stop the resistance movement, as India was looking for a seat in the UN Security Council and needed China's support.

In order to get the Tibetan resistance to surrender, the Dalai Lama sent a taped message to Mustang through his brother-in-law, PK Thakla. The taped message from the Dalai Lama acted like tinder in an already fraught situation, plagued by internecine divides. The Tibetan resistance was by then facing an upheaval within its ranks. That, coupled with a steady, aggressive and determined Nepalese army which had inside information about the fighters' movements, resulted in the Mustang camp caving in. It was a sad end. The resistance force that was a thorn in China's flesh ended in many suicides and encounter-deaths.

For Lhasang the collapse of Mustang and the suicide of his hero, Pachen, followed by the ambush marking the death of General Wangdu, a most revered commander, was a nightmare. A hush fell over McLeod Ganj and other Tibetan settlements. The Tibetans' one hope of getting back to their homeland was extinguished by the changed world order, crushed as Tibet was too insignificant to count on the world stage.

By 1974 it was all over. Back in McLeod Ganj, Lhasang felt he had been pushed off a cliff with no end in sight. He cried bitter tears, everything he had hoped and prayed for and modelled himself on was dead. He knew even his painstakingly written diary could bring peril, not just to him, but to many fighters who were either in prison or hiding in some remote corner. He sat down and burnt it page by page—the only account of one year as a resistance warrior.

At night while the world slept, he sat up wide-eyed; there was nothing to dream about anymore. An inner turmoil began eating him up. He felt some resentment at the Dalai Lama's role in sending the tapes. He wished he hadn't done that. But he knew it was done in all his wisdom.

The collapse of his world left a deep mark on him. He became agitated at the smallest of things and would lash out with angry words. Slowly, it became part of his personality.

A whole year passed. Then he got an unexpected offer to work as the Principal of the Tibetan Children's School. He had to earn, he had to move on with his life, so he accepted. He took the job and also got married. He oversaw the building of the school. That was when he encountered many silent men, who had once been guerrilla warriors and were now earning a living as labourers. From his office window and during his rounds, he would spot them standing over their shovels, looking at the horizon, their eyes still pools. He could not bring himself to check them to get back to work.

He started penning his thoughts, typing them out noisily on an old-fashioned typewriter in his spare time. His wife laughed at him saying his effort was like Columbus finding land, as his fingers hovered above the keys and his eyes searched for the alphabets. Daily usage brought proficiency. He also volunteered with the Tibetan Office of Research and Analysis, nicknamed TORA, the code word used by Japanese pilots in the bombing of Pearl Harbour. The office kept pace with international goings-on which the senior Tibetan leaders with their limited English language skills were unable to follow.

When the Dalai Lama encouraged the Tibetan youth to take part in more community affairs, Lhasang became the first President of the Tibetan Youth Congress, streamlining its Constitution and worldview. Impatient for change, he found it unbearable to continue with slow sonorous General Body Meetings when he wanted to create a consensus for the way forward for the Youth Congress. One meeting left him so frustrated that he stood up to sum up, 'I thank all participants but I think it's important that we don't lose sight of our goal. We all want Rangzen, freedom, a Free Tibet. It cannot be won on talks alone. Freedom is a country's life force that is paid not in gold and silver but with blood and gore.' He thumped his chest loudly to emphasize. His face grew red and agitated, suddenly he heard a gushing noise in his head and fell to the floor completely immobilized. For a minute no one in the hall reacted as he lay twitching on the floor, breathless, his eyes wild. Then people rushed to pick him up.

'Stay away, give him air, he is having an attack,' a young volunteer shouted. Lhasang was rushed to the nearest hospital. He had suffered a stroke. In a comatose state he was transferred to a hospital in Delhi, with doctors saying there was little hope he would pull through. But his brother was made of the same stuff as him. He drove Lhasang to Shimla and put him in the care of a Tibetan monk who started him on tantric treatment. Lhasang pulled through, coming out of his comatose state after three months. His long-term memory was crystal clear but his short-term memory took a beating. His brother laughed and told him he had survived because he had 'unfinished business of fighting for Tibet.'

He grinned back, 'Rangzen.'

But he came back to learn of the Five Point Peace Proposal, asking for restoration of peace and human rights in Tibet, put forth by His Holiness. The Tibetan Youth Congress examined, debated and lent it full support. The Chinese response was an outright rejection of the proposal. It only made Lhasang's resolve for Rangzen stronger in his heart.

The very next year in 1988, His Holiness came up with his Middle Way Approach whereby, while the Tibetans do not accept their present status under the People's Republic of China, they do not seek independence for Tibet. The Middle Way Approach, named after Buddhist philosophy, asked for Tibetan autonomy in the three traditional provinces of Tibet, allowing for complete freedom to preserve their culture, religion and national identity. In return the Tibetans gave up their right to seek freedom from China. The Middle Way thus gave China security, territorial integrity, and peaceful borders.

For Lhasang it was a shocking proposal. 'The Middle Way is unacceptable and unrealistic as it gives up the right to Tibetan freedom completely,' he argued. He started writing passionately of freedom being a life force—a nation not free was dead. The price for freedom was to be paid in the currency of blood and life, and unless this generation was willing to pay the price for their freedom the next generation would never be free, he wrote.

The many media interviews Lhasang gave against the Middle Way Approach made him an outcast in a tightly knit community. In public gatherings, friends and relatives looked surreptitiously away when he greeted them. At a meeting when he stood up to give his view, he found people leaving. Even many of those who started as revolutionaries agreed to the new peace path.

Faced with public anger and even threatened with death, Lhasang found he had unwittingly crossed a line. The Dalai Lama is the community's spiritual head and his word is law among his followers. There was no place for opposition to the views of His Holiness. Lhasang found himself isolated.

His wife of many years entreated him against such open dissent. When he did not stop, she preferred to cloister herself in a bookshop, knitting or telling her beads. By then their son was grown up with a family of his own.

Lhasang took himself off on long walks in the hills to preserve his sanity, coming back cold and exhausted, his heart heavy. He began writing down his arguments for Rangzen and he even met small groups of people, activists and desperate believers who felt that the Middle Way Approach was a blow to the Tibetan right to a free homeland.

If he could not free Tibet, he realized, he could at least visit it. Visas were hard to come by but not impossible. He made his plans, registered the bookshop in his wife's name and took a passage to Tibet. It was 1980 and China opened up Tibet for Tibetans who wanted to return or visit. He wanted to see if everything he had read about

Tibet and the reports pouring out from there were correct. He carried a camera and a small rucksack on his journey.

In Lhasa he saw the stark poverty of the Tibetans, with the Chinese always around and watchful of visitors. It was painful to hear young Tibetans speak only Chinese. He told those he could speak to of His Holiness and how the Tibetans lived in India. It was heart-breaking to see their eyes light up but fade out once he had finished.

Travelling in Tibet required special permits which took very long in coming. There was just one bus a month from Lhasa to Chamdo, traversing the dusty deserted plateau road. After waiting for days, he finally caught the bus and ran into an old Chushi Gangdruk warrior from Mustang. The two acknowledged each other with just a look.

During their many halts his friend told him he had become a carpet weaver and was based in Nepal. He was returning to meet his old mother. 'She is very ill. I hope she will be alive when I reach home,' he said. Lhasang said, 'I pray she will be.' His friend nodded his thanks. They were careful not to be seen talking too much.

When they reached Chamdo they were told to have their meals at a Chinese hotel. Not wanting to eat another Chinese meal he strolled down to the town square and saw a man selling apples.

He called out in Tibetan for the man to give him some apples, only to have a Chinese man hold them up and ask for the money in Chinese. Lhasang stood there feeling a cold dread. He didn't want to stay a single day in a Tibet which was full of Chinese. Frantically he turned away and went to pick up his rucksack from the bus. But his friend persuaded him to stay.

'Please don't go, you are the only one who has a camera. I want you to take a photo of my dying mother. It will be all I have.'

Lhasang nodded and walked home with his friend. He took the photos and stayed a month till the next bus came along and he got out of Tibet.

His family was eagerly awaiting his return. They crowded him as his wife gave him steaming ginger tea—he smiled, it was a far cry from the salted butter tea of Tibet. He sipped, savouring the warmth and feeling strangely at home.

'Well?' his wife prompted and he looked around, several pairs of curious eyes all waiting for his verdict. He sighed, 'We are a dying breed. You must tell everyone that at the rate the Chinese are flooding Tibet, we Tibetans will soon be extinct.'

His wife grimaced, 'Is that all you have come back with? Dismal predictions of impending doom.'

Lhasang sat quiet. When he could get an audience with His Holiness, he told him all that he saw in Tibet. Bowing low, he implored, 'I have been a volunteer before. I am ready to be sent anywhere. I have been waiting for orders and none have come.'

None came.

He was like a man who had been sentenced to the sidelines to watch the fate that would unfold with time.

Days changed to weeks, weeks to month and then to years; he and the margins merged. But the world around them began changing. In 2008, protests swept across Tibet, five decades after its occupation by China. Thousands were arrested while Tibetan monks, nuns, mothers, fathers, teenagers doused their clothes with kerosene and set themselves aflame, their dying cries, 'Long live Dalai Lama. Return the Precious Protector to Tibet. Free Tibet.' Desperate measures as they offered their bodies to chase away the darkness that surrounded their lives. Self-immolation was the last-ditch heroic measure of a despairing community who offered their flaming bodies as light in the profound darkness that surrounded their lives since Chinese occupation.

By 2008, Tibet's 2,100-year-old civilization was on the brink of extinction from the land of its origin. Its art and dance forms were mere caricatures in Chinese-run tourist resorts. The Tibetans had been trapped, forced to abandon their traditional nomadic existence and live in demarcated resettlements under constant surveillance of their movements by a repressive regime.

Everything Lhasang had feared for his homeland had come true. The demography of Tibet had changed and Sinicized completely. There were more Chinese than Tibetans in Tibet. Chinese was the medium of education and the official language of Tibet. Its vast natural and mineral resources worth billions of dollars were tapped and plundered.

Lhasang was desperate when the first reports of self-immolation began coming in. He got together with like-minded people, deeply saddened and helpless at the tragedies. 'They are paying for freedom with their lives. They are martyrs,' he said in a gathering that left the audience in tears. 'The last count is now 150 Tibetans who have died for Tibet. Our biggest tragedy is that we Tibetans, thanks to the Middle Way policy, have lost our clarity of purpose. Rangzen which should have been our goal has been changed to autonomy within Tibet that is ruled by the Chinese.' He paused, his dark eyes surveyed the crowd. 'We are like bricks scattered in a desert. All the bricks are not adding up. We want to build a home but we have no plan nor the land to build it on.

'We have a lot of foreign funders and celebrities supporting our cause, we are running campaigns and getting very good response. The latest campaign that is going worldwide is the global significance of the Tibetan plateau as the Third Pole—the water table of Asia and the Rainmaker. Tibet is the source of six main rivers that provide the much-needed irrigation waters to millions of farmers in the most densely populated nations, the life-giver of one fifth of the world's population. By using social media effectively, we have launched our global campaign and are certain these concerns with China's damming of all the rivers will affect and hold the world hostage. This is one way of forcing the world to pay attention and look at Tibetan issues.'

Lhasang looked around, his eyes riveted on an intense young man, who headed an NGO working on many campaigns for Free Tibet. He and young people like him were the new face of the Tibetan demand for freedom. He smiled. Just looking at the young man's earnest face, he felt that not everything was lost.

'True. But how effective are these campaigns without the blessings of His Holiness?' he questioned. He understood from years of being on the periphery that unless any movement had the hand of His Holiness over it, it would never get the world's attention or assent.

The young man paused, frowning as he looked up, 'Who would have thought the sun would set on the British Empire and that India would be free? Or that the Soviet Union would disintegrate into so many countries? History has shown that totalitarian regimes don't last forever. Communist China may not be able to stay that way with all its consumerism and no democracy. So while we wait for change we continue with our campaign to change people's perceptions and are ready when we get our chance.'

Lhasang gave a wry smile. These were arguments he would give to people who interviewed him. But it felt good that some young people were as passionate about Rangzen, that it burned as strong in their hearts too.

It was a nightly ritual for his wife to read a quote from her book on the Buddha. That night she read, 'From your suffering will come your happiness.' He had heard that one before, so he arched his eyebrows, muttering goodnight. 'Till then,' he said, 'I will dream of Tibet with my eyes closed.'

Amala

Tsamchoe Doma was brave, strong and broken—all at the same time.

I held her hand, my tears falling inside like incessant rain, watching her breathe as if willing her to take my breath and make hers stronger. The Rinpoche had gently said when he visited us at the ICU in hospital that she needed to be at home in peace. We got her off the ventilator, watching her all the way, hoping she realized she was home. She was in Kathmandu, the auspicious city she loved so dearly. It was here that she had spent much of her life.

Tsamchoe Doma—our mother, or Amala as we called her, was dying. Surrounded by her children, relatives, friends, lamas, and Rinpoches, it was a becoming farewell to an incredible woman who had dedicated seventy-two years of her life to others and never wanted anything in return.

When we reached home, Amala never opened her eyes. She was too far gone, as if she had already embarked on a journey where the illness could no longer touch her anymore. As I held her hand, frail and blue-veined, she gave it a gentle squeeze as if to say, 'I am alright, you take care.' I knew then that in the deepest recesses of her lost memory, she knew the journey that lay ahead of her.

Sonam Wangmo was the name Amala gave me when I was born: the same year she lost her homeland in Kalimpong, the place where my two elder brothers were studying in Missionary Schools. Amala's world had exploded in an exodus of bewildered and lost Tibetans fleeing their native land from the invading Chinese Army. In that chaotic time, she gave birth to me alone and with no one to lean on except her faithful maid Yangchen and a few Nepali helpers working with the family in Kalimpong.

I caress her hand and whisper a prayer into her ear. A prayer that she had taught me, reassuring her in my own way amidst the chants and prayer of the lamas as if providing her the directions of her journey, some comfort and consolation.

I recalled *The Tibetan Book of Living and Dying* that I had read and reread in the ICU. I took solace in the fact that only my mother's physical body was dying, but that her consciousness, or soul as some others term it, living in the diseased body would now be free. We Tibetans believe that our souls are timeless without beginning or end, moving from one life to the next until rebirth. Amala's consciousness was not her body and she would move on to a better space or body, preferably in Tibet where her heart lay.

Then the pulse meter stopped working. Amala was at peace. The outer dissolution where the five elements including her breath cease to function was over.

I held back my tears, pain and acute sense of loss and

instead asked that she be left alone and undisturbed to allow the peaceful inner dissolution of thoughts and emotions. As advised in the book, I tried hard to imagine her energy passing through a tunnel liberated from disease, anger and all other emotions, into Bhardo—the intermediary state that lasts at least forty-nine days until her consciousness moves on driven by the forces of karma.

I headed to nearby Pharbing to meet with her root guru—the Venerable Jhatu Rinpoche. The short drive felt like an eternity; crowded with memories of Amala, her gentle touch, her soft smile, our conversations, and her hugs that always felt like homecoming.

All gone.

I prayed to all the Gods I knew, leaving my mother's care now in their hands much like what she would have done. I whispered prayers softly in Tibetan over and over again. As she grew ill Amala reverted to her native tongue, Tibetan, refusing to speak any Nepali, Newari or Hindi that she knew so well, or the little English she spoke. It forced us all to reconnect with our Tibetan roots to become part of Amala's world.

As we drove, my husband marvelled at the slight drizzle and the brilliant rainbow that appeared as if out of nowhere, signalling to us that all was well. I embraced the thought. It eased my loss.

~

I was too young to know, but when I was old enough to ask her questions about the family, Amala told me that after giving birth she had recouped, impatiently regaining her strength and waiting for me to be strong enough to undertake the journey.

'Journey?' I had queried, and she had smiled. It lit up her face with all its oval planes and flamed up her agate coloured eyes. Amala was an arresting woman.

'Yes Bhomu, we went back to Tibet.' Even then, I knew Amala was a fiercely independent and spirited woman who lived life according to her terms, and once her mind was made there was very little that could change that.

My eyes are orbs, she has all my attention. Going back into Tibet when everyone was struggling to get away was no easy feat, nor recommended. Taking turns in carrying me tied to their back or hitching rides when available along with Yangchen who stood by my mother through thick and thin, Amala returned to Tibet to look for her family and complete unfinished business. She recounted how it took months as the two women followed an unknown route from Kalimpong to Lhasa, since the route Amala had taken out of Lhasa when she had come to meet her sons was unsafe and under heavy surveillance both from the Chinese and the Indian sides.

The usual facilities that existed on this route had been discontinued since the Chinese occupation, and it was completely closed in 1962 following the India-China war. They trekked from the early morning, resting by mid-morning and then continuing till evening, setting up camp for the night—always on their guard, hiding if they saw anything suspicious. They ate and drank sparingly, making sure to pick berries and leaves en route so that they did not run out of food, knowing well that if they ran out they would go hungry. Fortunately, money was not a problem for my mother, then a successful and wealthy businesswoman.

It would be close to six months before they reached their destination. 'Lhasa had changed,' recalled Amala, 'The Chinese were everywhere. Tibetans lived in constant fear, afraid of being picked up and imprisoned. Spies were everywhere and it was troubled, uncertain times.' All the houses in Lhasa were marked with chalk crosses as identification. Our house was untouched as the house of foreign nationals.

The peaceful life of freedom, laughter, harmony and spiritual bliss in Lhasa that my mother left behind was gone. The majority of Tibetans were compelled to abandon their homes and livelihoods and flee to neighbouring countries after the final overthrow of the Lhasa Government. Those left behind endured tremendous difficulties with family members being imprisoned and prosecuted by communist authorities for being feudal, bourgeois, religious or assisting the Tibetan government or its causes. Brother was pitted against brother, children against parents and domestic help against their former employers.

Then the Chinese forces took the decision to liberate Tibet. First, by taking over the geographical territory of Tibet; second, by winning over the Tibetans in freeing them from their religious and class-based ideologies. They expected unanimous support from the people of Tibet whom they considered suppressed and oppressed. But their plans for the Tibetans backfired—what they had never envisaged was that the Tibetans were fiercely independent and proud of their identity, country and religious affiliations, including respect and total loyalty for Kundun or His Holiness (HH) Dalai Lama. Outbreaks of rebellion took place in Kham and Amdo and ultimately Lhasa. The outcomes were violent measures, and the use of force and military strength, propaganda campaigns and mass socialist reforms were aimed to secure China's position in Tibet.

The international response to all of this, including that of neighbouring India and Nepal as well as others like Britain that had long histories of association and representation in Tibet, was wary of compromising their interests and ruining relations with the new communist China. In return China allowed foreign nationals, including Indians and Nepalis, to exit Tibet and secure their possessions. Amala felt secure with a Nepali shield, as she was married to a Nepali man and settled into her old home. Her mission in Lhasa was to find her now lost and scattered extended family and friends; alongside gathering and consolidating her transportable belongings and funds to send to her husband in Nepal.

She attended all the mandatory public prosecutions and speeches, aided by her one-time close help Tenzing who had now become an important officer working for the Chinese. The pain, grief, suffering and loss were unbearable. I can only imagine how Amala must have tried to survive and stay safe, keeping Yangchen and me protected in her occupied homeland. At the age of twenty-four, mother-of-three Amala turned grey overnight. Her beautiful long black silken hair was shrouded in silver.

Getting into Tibet was much easier than getting out. She sought the help of the Nepalese counsellor and other foreign friends including the Indian Counsel to transport some of her assets to Nepal. Additionally, she needed permits to allow the three of us—Amala, Yangchen and myself—to travel to Nepal. It took a year or so...what seemed like eternity then.

~

History has it that following the marriage of a Nepali princess, Bhrikuti, with the Tibetan King Songtsan Gompo in the seventh century, Newari (ethnic Nepali people from Kathmandu) traders and artisans established business in major cities of Tibet and operated between Nepal and Tibet for centuries. The trans-Himalayan trade that existed from the medieval period to this century added significant dimensions to Nepal-Tibet relations. They used caravan routes consisting of porters, mules, donkeys and yaks as transport from borders of North Nepal (Kyirong, Kuli) into Tibet which was a more difficult journey, and later in the 1930s new routes between Tibet and Sikkim (via Gangtok and Kalimpong) opened up.

My father's family had been trading between Tibet and Nepal, bringing into Tibet finished products like metals, textile and rice and carrying back into Nepal and India yak wool and gold dust. Daya Bir, my father, was the oldest boy of a landed and wealthy Newari family that was also engaged in helping mint gold coins in Nepal for the previous Tibetan government. It was Daya Bir's first trip away from home at the young age of sixteen, and circumstances required long stays and travel during that time. He learned Tibetan, fell in love with and married a young Tibetan girl, Tsamchoe Doma, with total abandon for his culture, society and the future consequences of his actions—including withholding pertinent information about himself. All seemed fair in love at the time.

Amala's father, my Popo-la, was a highly respected Ngapa, a tantric Buddhist practitioner, assigned to the office of HH the Dalai Lama to perform prayers to invoke rain and even to stop it. Growing up in traditional Tibetan family from Shigatse and Lhasa, Amala grew up steeped in the Buddhist ways. She was sixteen when, rescuing some animals from a butcher's shop in Lhasa's crowded market place, she first encountered the young handsome Newari boy from Nepal, Daya Bir. While she was bargaining for the price to save one or at most two animals from slaughter, this young Newari boy bought out all the animals from the butcher and asked Tsamchoe Doma what she planned to do with them. Little did he realize that she was the daughter of Kusho Chokpala, who was well-known for running voluntarily one of the largest animal shelters in Lhasa, where even HH Dalai Lama would visit and bless.

Bewildered by his generosity and kindness, she befriended him; he was completely smitten with Amala' beauty, simplicity and courage. They met often and fell in love, much to the horror of her conservative family. For her religious and traditional family, he was a Chegyal—a foreigner and a transient trader. Marrying an outsider was considered sacrilege. But Amala was determined that he was the man she would marry, as all the Tibetan men being proposed or married to like her sisters were 'noble men' or 'religious men' but their interests, as Amala's young mind saw, were limited to picnics, gambling and ladies.

Amala had ambitions of her own, including seeing the world; she wanted more from life. In fact, travelling to Beijing with a Chinese cousin for a few months where she was exposed to art, pottery—porcelain and cloisonné making and glazes—was the high point in her life then. She also admired the very few beautiful Tibetan aristocratic ladies who studied in faraway places and spoke foreign languages, and the Indian Counsellor's wife who taught her a few foreign words and treated her like a daughter.

Defying her family, she married the Nepali man who promised her the moon and more, and the two set up home in Lhasa. Father spent long periods of time between Nepal and Lhasa, and later Kalimpong as that was the time it took for the caravan to travel to and fro. Happily, they raised two sons.

Amala had begun travelling to Kalimpong and Calcutta as well, and started her own business trading in luxury goods like Yardley soaps, West End and Rolex watches, razors, make-up and brocade. She now had the opportunity to have her children educated in English, much like some of the people in Lhasa she admired. Her two boys were sent to schools in Kalimpong where she stayed at a house called Lhasa Villa. Life could not have been better. Her family had forgiven her after her sons were born. Amala delighted in buying presents and gifting her mother and siblings—they were a large family of eleven—and she also helped to pay off her gambling aristocratic brother-in-law's debts. She was a star and in demand in Lhasa, especially among the noble ladies who were her customers and friends. Saola, as she called my father, adored his wife and was the best husband and father anyone could have hoped for and much than she imagined. Life seemed too good to be true.

~

Amala stayed on in Kalimpong for an extended period of time to see and be around her two boys while Father returned to Lhasa with the intention of going on to Nepal and bringing up a caravan of goods. That was all Amala knew when she returned to Lhasa with me. She had left her business and home in the care of her younger unmarried sister Dickyla who lived with her and whom she looked after in Lhasa.

While Amala settled in to wait, hoping to receive her travel permit, she was able to ensure that Dickyla and one of her younger brothers, Thupten, with the help of a Newari salesperson she had earlier employed, travelled to Nepal. During her absence nothing had been taken from her house but the roof was strewn with discarded guns, dumped by Tibetan fighters whose lives and houses were raised; they were fleeing the Chinese army. Anyone caught with guns was executed immediately. So Amala and the maid were forced to undertake the dangerous mission of disposing off the guns in the best ways they knew, or facing death. Within the context of grave fear, persecution, imprisonment and death among her fellow Tibetans, Amala at great risk to herself allowed her home to be used as a hiding place and shelter to those needing protection, including monks and nuns and victims of torture and rape. She immersed herself in caring for them clandestinely while waiting and praying for papers from her husband to help her get out of Tibet.

Her own quest to find her larger extended family and relatives drew a blank. When she was finally able to exit Tibet with help from friends and well-wishers—as the papers from my father never arrived—she wept for the country and the city of her birth, the relatives, friends and other Tibetans she was leaving behind, not knowing whether she would ever see them or what her own fate and theirs would be. It was the saddest day and time of her life and she prayed to the famous Jokhang in Lhasa to protect her country and bring peace to its people, who had never harmed anyone including the Chinese.

Once she reached Kathmandu, she found my father's home in the heart of the city in a buzzing area called Asan and so we were finally reunited with him.

~

Knocking on the ornately carved door, Amala stood on the threshold of the traditional Newari home. Father was there and so was his whole family. Years later I tried to imagine how Amala must have appeared to the conservative Newari family, travel-worn and carrying me, then over two years old, in her arms. By then Nepal had been inundated with Tibetans. The 'Bhottes,' as Nepalese called Tibetan refugees, were looked down upon; Amala too must have appeared in similar light to father's family: a lone young woman who claimed she was their son's wife and had borne him three children. Father had never told his family of his marriage earlier, but with the Chinese occupation of Lhasa and closure of trade including from Kalimpong, Amala's return to Tibet and the hiatus that followed, he decided to inform his family about his Tibetan family and bring his two sons to Kathmandu.

To call it a paradigm shift would be an understatement. Amala's world shattered further when not only were she and her daughter unwelcome in this traditional joint family that my father was a part of, but he was also already married to a shy young Newari woman who lived in their house. The family members, however, were intrigued and curious and they had little choice but to accept us into their lives, much like how they had responded to the two young boys that arrived from Kalimpong. All the struggles and hardship did not match up to the joy my mother felt at being reunited with her two boys who were adjusting to their new life—from being the adored darling boys of the family, to outcastes and unwelcome additions in Father's family, without a mother. The boys were ecstatic to be with Amala again and to see me for the first time. Amala's sorrows and pain were buried against the pleasures of being reunited with her children, and she had little choice but to accept her circumstances. She consoled herself with the thought that she had much to be thankful for and her situation was better than many others in Tibet and in Nepal.

Amala never spoke too much about this phase in her life, but when I piece it all together from remembered memory of what I heard her say, I can only imagine Amala's life. The betrayal she must have felt at Father not telling her about his first wife, or not coming clean with his family that he had married in Tibet. I am sure she felt resentment at him for not sending her travel papers and leaving her to her fate in her occupied homeland, where victors ruled as they willed. She did understand that he had no choice as a child to marry, in his family's ancient tradition. Although his traditional marriage had not been consummated and Father told Amala she was the only woman he had ever loved, to adjust to a new life governed by all the traditional Newari ways chafed. The Tibetan and Nepalese ways were a world apart.

From the matriarchal system that Amala came from, where women were independent and inheritors of property, she entered into a rigidly patriarchal system where a woman's standing at every level was contingent on her husband or her parents. The Newari household was embedded in caste and stringent rules juxtaposed between Buddhist and Hinduism. The Saes (Newari word for Tibetans) were treated as janjati. Amala and I joined our brothers in the segregated space allocated to us to live and eat separately from the rest of the family. My brothers often objected, especially the older one who refused to wash his own plate after a meal or stay within confined spaces, resulting in severe punishment. Amala always intervened and got abused as well.

Amala tried initially but caved in from the endless discrimination, restrictions and emotional discomfort. Father's younger brother and other members of the family were curious and kind to Amala and us. There were also Newari relatives and visitors who sympathized with us as Amala struggled to learn the language and challenge the cultural oppression of women being confined to the household. One bright spark was that Amala reunited with her sister Dickyla and brother Thupten. As fate would have it, Dickyla had married and set up home in Patan with the very salesperson who had accompanied her from Lhasa. Amala's brother Thupten had fallen in love with a Gurung girl from Bhoudha who gave him shelter and married him. These were unusual times.

~

Amala realized that she had to leave this constricting environment to be of any use to herself or her family, especially her children. She was keen to get her sons back into English schools and persuaded my father to do so. With the help of other people, my older brother went to boarding school in Kathmandu while my second brother was sent to a local school nearby. Any other woman given her hopeless situation and three children would have succumbed to the weight of her circumstances, or destiny as some may call it. But not Amala. She did the unthinkable and asked for separation. Father did everything in his means to stop her from leaving.

'Was it because Father had not sent for you for so many years that you wanted to separate?'

She was quiet as if she had taken each word and weighed it. She had shaken her head and replied, 'No. I know his first wife had no way out as she had never seen the world outside her home or taken life's hard knocks. I had. I didn't want to build my happiness on her unhappiness and I also could not be in a relationship with a man with two wives. Once married, a Newari woman cannot return to her parents and must obey her husband irrespective of the abuse she might be going through. I had no other choice and I did not want you to go through that.'

I didn't understand it at the time, but later I have often wondered: what would have become of my life had I lived with my father?

That was when the Newari Guthi (traditional clan heads) stepped in and sanctioned their separation, awarding Amala a sum of sixty thousand rupees but no right over her children. In their judgement, they felt the children would be safer and better taken care of as Father's family was well-reputed and rich and they would provide well for the children. My mother was a refugee with little means and family support. My father also denied receiving any of the things from Tibet that she had painstakingly sent through transport and trusted people.

By then I was already three. Amala sought the help of a Tibetan cousin and my older brother to steal me from my father's home. I have only a vague memory of struggling and trying to fight off someone's tight grip. It was my cousin commandeering the help of my eldest brother who lured me to the doorway. Amala's cousin whisked me off to her. We were on the first bus out from Kathmandu to Kalimpong. That was where Amala left me while she worked to rebuild her life. She enlisted me in the nursery of the convent school my brother had gone to, but left me initially in the care of a Tibetan monk and later at Mrs King's home as I was too young to be taken in as a boarder. Seeing my mother's plight and remembering her from her old days, Reverend Mother Cecelia became my surrogate mother de facto. She would often recount that I was one of the youngest children she has taken into boarding and that I was no bigger than her little finger when she first saw me. I spent many happy years of my life there, including during the holidays together with only the sisters and sometimes a good-looking priest when on retreat.

Amala moved back to Nepal to take care of my brothers, especially to get my middle brother into a boarding school, but fate had other things in store for her and she moved back to Kalimpong to take care of one of her older sister Dolkarla's little children. Their mother who fled into Sikkim was taken by the Indian Government and sent to Rajasthan, suspected of being a Chinese spy. Amala used everything she had and worked hard to secure the release of her sister from Rajasthan and ensure that her children were taken care of during this vulnerable period. The three boys were sent to the same school my brothers had gone to, and the little girl joined me in the convent.

Slowly Amala got her life back. Dolkarla was subsequently vindicated and released from Rajasthan; Amala helped her to settle in Kathmandu where the rest of the family members were. Years after Amala's death my two brothers spoke for the first time of the resentment they harboured against her for taking only me and for leaving them behind to look after my cousins. I am not sure why Amala did that. But I can only presume that she felt she had little to offer the boys. By staying with their father, they would assimilate into the Nepali culture, learn his ways and later join in his business as well as get their rightful inheritance. I had no answer to their question of why Amala took me with her. I think it must have been because she had to have something to live for and I was too young to leave behind, or a girl child in the confines of a Newari household.

Our home in Nepal was never just the two of us. Although my brothers were forbidden to visit their mother since they officially lived with our father, Amala's home was for all of us. She made their beds and cooked for them every day. Nothing could keep my brothers from visiting her whenever they could. They called her 'Tibetan-mom.' In fact, my brothers were the apple of her eyes. I came home for the winter holidays sometimes and slowly bit-by-bit she built a safe world for all of us.

~

It was once in the winter break that I came home to a lot of noise. There were a lot of people in the house. As Amala's business stabilized, she started keeping an open house. I often resented her ways as our home was always open to visitors and those in need. Usually it was my room that was sacrificed and I was expected to adjust and share with others my space, books, clothes or the toys I had. If I protested and threw a tantrum, Amala would say in a voice that brooked no argument. 'Bhomu you have no choice— either you can choose to be happy sharing or miserable and sharing—but sharing you must do in this house. They are people who need help and many have helped us. Now it is our turn to give back.'

As a teenager I met cousin Drechen from Tibet who came to stay with us. We called her Semla as she was a princess by birth. She stayed over and Amala insisted that I help out, so I helped her bathe, wash out her lice-ridden hair and throw away her foul-smelling travel clothes. On Amala's insistence, I took her sightseeing around Kathmandu reluctantly. We took in some sights and landed up in a fancy restaurant for tea.

The waiter arrived with our teas and a platter of pastries. I took one and asked Drechen to choose one for herself.

Drechen looked at the delicate cream and chocolate glazed pastries, her eyes enormous in delight. 'Can I have all of them?' The waiter nodded leaving the platter at our table. I was mortified. Why did Amala's relatives have to be so coarse?

'Ola, do you think I can pack them and take them home?'

'Home? Amala is not very fond of sweets.'

She gave me an embarrassed smile, 'No Ola, I didn't mean your home. I meant I want to take them back to Tibet with me. I want to take them for my family there. I have never seen something so beautiful. I feel guilty eating these sweets without them.'

I nodded, stumped. I knew for sure the pastries wouldn't survive the journey to Tibet which took months. 'You eat one at least.' She nodded. Her enthusiasm in everything was childlike, although she was in her late teens and years older than me. I looked across as she took a bite of the pastry, her eyes closing in delight at its exquisite flavour. She smiled, her eyes lighting up. Drechen was a beautiful woman with long hair and delicate features that made her stand out anywhere in a crowd.

'Tell me about your home.' Almost immediately her eyes clouded over. It was like a bright sun had suddenly got eclipsed by dark clouds. She spoke softly of their lives, the constant fear of repression from the Chinese, the imprisonment of relatives for no comprehensible reason. Once in prison they never came back. Her voice trembled as she spoke of the hopelessness of their poverty and having to eke out a living as labour in their own land, the continual fear of what a new day would bring. The more she spoke, the more alarmed I felt.

'Don't be afraid, you are safe here,' she said with a smile. I didn't know that my eyes had teared over. 'God willing, I will be safe too. I will be marrying the most wonderful man and we will have enough to eat and not starve. He is kind and has a job.'

'What does he do?'

'He is a driver; he drives a truck for the government. Jobs are impossible for Tibetans unless you have some qualification or skill they need.'

I sat there stunned—a princess marrying a driver. I looked across at Drechen afraid for what would become of her.

She became my turning point.

~

When I met my Popo-la, a man with piercing eyes and so much power and presence, and my mother's other siblings and their husbands in Nepal, I was much more prepared.

'Bhomu, prostrate before your Popo-la.'

Popo-la took my hands into his and kissed them. He and a few of Amala's siblings had managed to escape in a large group and make it out of Tibet. It was a cause for celebrations. They were alive and together. No one spoke of those who were left behind. When the Chinese had overtaken Tibet, Popo-la had moved to a monastery which was a two-day-walk from Lhasa, and so had not been able to join the mass exodus of 1959 as the Chinese had sealed all borders. It was also one of the reasons why Amala had not been unable to locate them. At Kathmandu in Amala's small flat, everyone felt they were lucky to be alive and together.

After a few days with us Popo-la moved out and began to live in Boudha with his daughter Dickyla and her husband; Amala's other siblings too settled down close by. She now had emotional support. The family drew strength from each other and we celebrated Losar together. But I would constantly see Amala warding off suggestions of another marriage that Popo-la insisted was best for her.

'Don't tell me what's best for me Pala, I have lived and made my own destiny,' Amala would retort, her eyes like a winter storm.

But Popo-la would look at Amala and say softly, 'Not every man will betray you. You are young and in an alien country away from your home, you need to be married to stay safe.' It was a difficult time for Tibetan women where their ways were considered available; a lot of exploitation, rape and abuse was taking place. Divorced women had no place really in Nepali society at that time. Tibetan women were also lured as the local people soon realized that most Tibetans possessed some gold, jewellery and other assets that could be exploited. Every day a new horror story would emerge among the community as it struggled to survive.

It would be months before Popo-la's will prevailed and Amala married a flamboyant Khampa a few years younger to her. My new father had first met Amala in Lhasa market and pursued her, but she had rejected him insisting he should concentrate on girls his age. He had seen her again in Kalimpong when she went to his school to visit my cousins, and then he made his way to Kathmandu to meet my grandfather. In the changed circumstances they married—Amala to please her father, him for love.

It wasn't much of a match. Life's hard knocks had made Amala turn inwards. She had developed tremendous self-control and even when she was in pain or angry, she kept it all harnessed inside, saying only that much in her quiet contained way. Pala was a simple man, but highly educated in Tibetan and also with knowledge of English having spent a few years in the missionary school in Kalimpong. Despite our initial resistance towards this person who had entered our mother's life, we all learned to accept and love him as he had the biggest heart imaginable and never let anyone feel excluded or unwanted. He was a complete foil to Amala and it was with great trepidation that she gave birth to my younger brother when I was nine.

Pala got a job with the Tibetan Refugee Centre in Nepal translating Tibetan documents into English while Amala focused on running a small business. She became one of the most respected art collectors in Nepal, selling her collection selectively to key people in Nepal and travelling on business to the UK, Hong Kong, Thailand and Malaysia. My first foreign trip was with my mother to Hong Kong where I was amazed at her abilities to handle Chinese buyers and speak in Chinese. We brought back luxury goods, silk and western clothes to sell in Nepal. Her collection of rugs bought from Tibetan and other travellers was one of the best I had seen. Our house was like a living museum where her clients from India, Europe and elsewhere visited and bought stuff. She was a businesswoman par excellence.

It was a golden age as far as our family was concerned, and Kathmandu was at its best before the congestion and pollution had hit the city. It was a haven for tourists— the city was green all around, surrounded by visible and beautiful snow-capped mountains. Its inhabitants were simple and accommodating, enjoying the small things in life where values and spirituality were premium. Every corner of Kathmandu was special with its temples and statues. The architecture and craftsmanship were one of the best in the world. Old palaces and buildings alike were marvels juxtaposing traditional centuries-old Nepalese art and architecture with colonial style buildings and art borrowed from Europe during the Rana regime. Amala loved gardening and had green fingers. We lived in an old Rana palace in the heart of the city which had one of the best gardens that we could boast about. Reporters and artists would come to take pictures and draw the landscape of our green space.

Clearly, she was a woman ahead of her times, breaking all barriers and setting the trend and example for many women of that era to follow. This is reflected in the respect and love she earned and enjoyed within the community, both Tibetan and Nepali, where she arbitrated family disputes, helped arrange marriages and raise funds for those in need. Her experiences in Tibet and Nepal helped shape her passion for justice. She advocated for women and had a meticulous desire to make women's lives better. She regularly signed me up as a volunteer to help weaker students or work with the Nepal Woman Association where many battered women took shelter.

It was only after Amala had passed away, when we retraced our connections, that I was surprised to learn how Pala had dedicated his life to working for the Tibetan cause and was fiercely loyal to His Holiness whom he had followed in escaping to India. He had moved to Nepal because of our mother. Our life in Kathmandu was idyllic even though Amala had become extremely frugal and insecure following her life experiences; unwilling to experiment, take risks with work or life, including investing in property or expanding her business. Everything was transient for her and she had made a firm commitment to spirituality and service. She would focus her energies into work and helping others, including Nepali women who were battered or thrown out from their homes, and Tibetans trying to make a semblance of their lives. A substantial percentage of anything she earned was given away. This self-imposed tax later resulted in conflict with her children who disagreed with her approach. Resources were required to expand the business or for other purposes. She refused to budge from her position, creating rifts in the family with my brothers moving on to start their own lives. I supported my mother unconditionally, too young then to really understand.

~

I was in constant awe of my mother and also very fearful of her commanding ways. I supported her emotionally and financially when I was able. I remember her sacrifices and the way she cared for us and others. Her father, Popo-la, passed away in Kathmandu in my aunt's house. The family members were gathered there. I thought we were having a family party, but unknown to the children my grandfather had decided to leave his body and depart into another world, from where he would never return to this world in any form. His sons were unable and unwilling to take on the practice of Ngapa and thus was the end of a lineage that had seen many generations...The lineage of Ugen Pema Rinzen of the Ngingma tradition.

Following Popo-la's demise, Amala decided she wanted to get into more serious religious practice and asked to be separated from Pala. He moved on reluctantly to India while Amala started balancing her time between the family, work and dharma. She was loved by all but most importantly by all the lamas and Rinpoches with whom she interacted regularly. Her two sons had grown into young adults, having returned after completing their studies in the UK and Germany. Our younger brother was in boarding school in India. I stayed home with Mother, helping her and then starting my own business. The golden era of our family life in Kathmandu continued—safe and friendly.

Amala was the tree under which I flourished. I finally began to understand my powerful and complex mother, appreciating her candour and intimacy in recounting life's mysteries and stories to me. Too many to get into here, but they were an inspiring testament to her extraordinary determination and power of believing in oneself. She nurtured and ensured that she sowed the seeds of compassion, love and acceptance in her children.

She had never had a formal English education but when I was growing up, she set targets for me every day. When I began doing well in studies, she would send me to teach summer English classes at the Tibetan school. Almost all the children there were orphans or from very poor backgrounds. It was her way of showing me how lucky I was. Every day I would watch my washing powder for clothes diminish, till I found out that the girls were stealing it to wash their hair that glistened like black silk in the sun. But that summer I could cross the bridge and understand what it means to be a refugee in a land where dreams could also come true.

Like my mother I too wanted to see more of the world. I decided to leave and pursue my studies abroad, and as fate would have it, a scholarship from a US university sealed the deal. My mother was not happy to see me go but she understood my curiosity and desire to travel and learn, and that I was outgrowing Kathmandu. I promised to return after my studies, and she was proud and happy to see me graduate. She was an instant hit among my friends and professors who found her charming, smart and cultured.

By then my younger brother too finished school and moved to the US for studies. Amala would give a contented smile and say that finally she could rest a bit as all her children had started out on their own paths. One of the best times in my life was the six months Amala and I spent together in the US travelling between Boston, New York, Washington and California, following which she returned to Nepal and I accepted a job at an international NGO working with refugees.

In an unspoken way, what I had seen Amala endure as a refugee and how she had found ways to help people became a benchmark for me—my job with the international NGO was the perfect way to make a difference in a world that was sharply divided between the developed and still developing countries.

With the NGO I embarked on a journey of possibilities and worked with like-minded people. I was humbled and proud at the same time to be the first among many Tibetans and Nepalis to be able to make useful contributions, not only for my people but for many other people from uprooted and war-torn contexts from around the world. I felt grateful having found my raison d'etre to give back to the world that had given me so much. Amala's legacy also lives on through my brothers who have inherited her tenacity for hard work and compassion and become successful professionals in their own rights. Two of them have made substantial investments from their savings in social and health related projects to make the lives of poor people better, especially those in Nepal. Her youngest son, living and working in New York, supports old age homes in Kalimpong and Nepal for Tibetans. Like her, all her children are well-travelled, having lived in several continents and on their terms.

~

Unknown to us all, our lives were about to change.

Amala decided to go to back to Tibet to connect with her roots after more than thirty years. Nothing any of us said could make her change her mind. Popo-la had died some years ago, there was no one strong enough to prevail on Amala. So off she went to Tibet. With all her children well taken care of, she felt the time was right for her to do the things that mattered most to her. She missed her country and its people and wanted to revisit her childhood and other memories that she had left behind. She was confident that the Jokhang that she had prayed to while leaving Lhasa would give her an opportunity to return again one last time. Her prayers were answered and she got her visa to travel to Tibet.

This was in the 1990s and Lhasa had changed yet again. On surface the people had adjusted their ways to meets the new demands of the communist regime and life was carrying on with its usual hustle and bustle for most people. However, underlying the surface, there was continued fear and deprivation and neglect of Tibetan people. The Tibetan language—its intonation and vocabulary—had undergone subtle changes to include Chinese. Young people dressed in blue pants and jackets almost like they were in a national uniform, looked happy, pretending to be Chinese movie stars with curly hair and thin eyebrows. There were bars and brothels everywhere frequented by the Tibetan youth. Simultaneously, the Jokhang and other holy sites were inundated with people doing prostrations and burning incense as in the past on special days in spite of the fear. It was post the cultural revolution, but for the Tibetans and Tibet it was still grey times with curfew. The underlying currents were heavy.

Amala did not return to Nepal as planned. She was expected to return in three months but three years had passed. I pulled every string in my repertoire and visited Lhasa to meet her and bring her back with me. I found Amala in a housing complex that the Chinese had built in the heart of Lhasa called Bhagor where the majority of the Tibetans lived in ghetto-like situations. Since her old house had been destroyed to build these new structures, she was given a corner complex comprising three floors as compensation. Likewise, many other Tibetan-Nepalis were also allowed to keep their properties and continue trading between Nepal and Tibet via Thato Pani, the border town linking the two countries. New roads had been built connecting the two countries and making transportation and trade easier.

Amala had found some of her relatives, while others had not survived and some could not be accounted for. She was happy meeting with old friends and relatives in Lhasa, travelling to her hometown in Shigatse, spending time in her home in the Bhagor and they say old habits die hard. She was surrounded by people in need and constantly short of money. While on the surface she seemed fine, she had lost weight and looked somewhat frail; a little casual about her appearance and with money, which was very unusual given her frugal nature. I was a little perplexed at this changed attitude and behaviour, including in the way she handled her visa. My mother whom I knew as a strict, well-organized, hard-working person setting high standards for herself and others had changed.

I didn't dwell much on those issues as I assumed that the altitude, quality of life and unknown stress must have impacted her and she was more relaxed now. Everything would be fine once she returned to the comforts of her home and life in Kathmandu. With the help of friends, we organized her exit visa so that she could return to Nepal. We flew back to Kathmandu together leaving her house, belongings and papers in the care of her friend Wangyal.

Little did we know that life would never be the same.

~

When Amala returned to Nepal she found that her flourishing business had come to a halt in the past three years. She was keen to restart but my brothers felt that it was probably best that she retired and enjoyed the remaining part of her life without stress and responsibilities. She agreed reluctantly but her life as she knew it changed dramatically and no one could have predicted what was in store for her.

She became restless, unpredictable, moody, emotional and sometimes mean. Amala's two oldest help, who had raised us as children and who had been with her ever since, were sent back home to Kalimpong to their families with large sums of money for their old age. In fact, they had been waiting for over three years for her in Nepal. They cried, protested and begged to remain but Amala insisted that she now needed to live alone.

Relatives living in Nepal noted that Amala was missing her children. The beautifully dressed and meticulous woman who was always colour coordinated and conscious of her looks no longer seemed to care. She was the one who used to spray her sheets with expensive perfume and was very particular about personal hygiene. Her otherwise well-maintained house now was getting a little neglected. She stopped cooking and entertaining friends and became somewhat of a recluse, wandering off from the wee hours of the morning to late nights to temples, monasteries and homes of relatives and friends unannounced. Other than that, and repeating herself in conversations, she appeared completely normal.

She lived on her own and continued with her religious practices and routines; to the relatives and friends that did visit her there was nothing out of the usual. I would call her regularly and she did complain of getting old and not being able to remember things too well, but nothing to cause any alarm. Any insecurities she may have felt, or loss of motivation and self-care, or apathy she hid well. Occasionally, a relative would call and complain that Amala was behaving very strangely and had mistreated them, or that she refused to clear an old account. I discounted everything I heard, knowing my mother and the nonconformist that she was. She was being unduly targeted by others as a difficult old lady.

Her disarming persona and soft gentle and charming ways ultimately melted everyone's hearts and we all learned to accept her the way she was. It was my husband who noticed while visiting Amala and having to make tea for himself that the kitchen was unused. He tried to place a new help to work for her but she refused, resulting in him sending her meals prepared in his home every day. What was unusual was that the tiffins were often returned unopened. She also regularly misplaced keys and locked herself out of her home, whereupon my husband was always called upon to help. What was disconcerting was that she did not seem to recall these instances, or pretended they did not happen. In retrospect I can only imagine how difficult this must have been for her. Thinking that a change of scene would be good for Amala, he somehow persuaded her to travel with him to the US to visit me.

It was almost as if she let her guard down when she saw me and my younger brother in New York. She confided in me with tears in her eyes that she could no longer remember her prayers and that she wanted me to come back to Nepal to live with her as she was getting old. She often threw tantrums and refused to have her meals or stay indoors. It was then that it dawned on me that Amala needed help. Something was not quite right. I forced her to undergo medical tests which failed to reveal much initially, but we persisted in taking her to the best specialists and ultimately honed it down to some form of dementia—maybe of the Alzheimer's type.

We finally understood her agitation, stubbornness, constant travel—they were the cry of a fading mind clutching at what she remembered and was familiar with, before even that merged with the ocean of blank her memory was becoming. Her compelling, direct and funny ways would slowly fade. This was one of the most difficult times for her and me. It was hard to see her go from a seemingly independent, vivacious and driven woman to leading a constrained and dependent life. I knew she would need 24/7 care and decided that her family would provide that care.

She was my best friend and closest confidante as well as my fiercest critic and shrewdest advisor. How would we cope with the disease and insecurity and uncertainty it brings with it? How do we overcome the sense of hopelessness and frustration?

I moved often throughout my career and Amala and her home in Kathmandu represented the elements of stability in my life. I remember our home always decorated with plants and flowers and the smell of incense with my mother there—the high energy, fashionable, beautiful and fun-loving woman. I desperately wanted to have that strong and feisty woman with distinct Tibetans sayings she was never short of, her lessons and laughter in my life.

I moved back to Asia to ensure Amala's new living environment and lifestyle for her safety and well-being. Up until the very end, it was difficult for anyone to know on the surface that Amala was not well. She always greeted people with a smile and some kind words and the family provided her the best that money could buy in terms of care. My house revolved around Amala and what she needed, as she gradually moved into a state of second childhood with the progression of the disease. The loss I felt when our roles were reversed with me becoming the caretaker and her the child was unfathomable. I was devastated, but adjusted with the knowledge that she was still there and giving me an opportunity to share our lives. While she was dependent on caregivers and spoke little, somewhere deep in me I knew she understood. She could return emotional signals.

While she could have stayed with my older brother who was based in Nepal at the time, I insisted on her living with me. It was time for me to move again but this time with Amala and some caregivers. Everything was packed and shipped but Amala never left Nepal. Somehow, she did not want to travel yet again or had lost the will to continue to live. She deteriorated swiftly and had to be hospitalized. It was as if she wanted to move on.

My expatriate home in the new designated duty station was a large bungalow built in traditional colonial style with a wraparound verandah and sprawling garden with willows and unusual flowers. Amala would have loved it. Forty-nine days after the last rituals, I had moved alone. As I unpacked the baggage sent earlier with Amala's clothes, medicines and the empty wheelchair… I felt a lump in my throat and tried to contain my tears, wondering where she was.

I have often wondered about the human spirit and

resilience and what our Amala taught us unwittingly—the importance of perseverance and faith and remaining human amidst tragedy. She moved forward and built a successful life, a life well-lived and blessed as Rinpoche noted—it is only very special people that get a chance to wash off all their negative karma in this life; her displacement and illness provided her that opportunity and the possibility to her children as well, to rise up to the occasion and care deeply.

Tsamchoe Doma was indeed blessed.

In the eternal cycle of life, I know her blessings live on in us...

Author's Note

MY INTRODUCTION TO the Tibetans started unexpectedly with a phone call from a stranger who spoke with a French accent. He had read some of the stories I had done for *The Hindu* as a freelancer and had got my phone number from their office. He asked if we could meet as he was in Delhi, so we met. He was a Canadian photographer who showed me some amazing black-and-white photos of Tibetan men and women living in an Old Age Home called Jampaling in McLeod Ganj, Dharamshala, India.

I loved his photographs; they were powerful and moving. I told him he should do a photo feature for a magazine. He said that he could not write and asked if we could team up. So one weekend I travelled to McLeod Ganj with Francois and his girlfriend Marie.

We spent a whole day at Jampaling—me with my notebook and him with his camera. A young Tibetan man translated for us. Most of what I heard left me in tears. I wrote the story 'Jampaling' and sent it with some of Francois's pictures to an international magazine. Sadly, they said they had a long waiting list and the story was never published.

'Jampaling' stayed in my computer. Instead I began

writing the book that had written itself inside me, *The Keeper of Memories*, a historical fiction work on the Gorkhas. After the book was published, I began wondering what to work on next. That's when 'Jampaling' showed up in my computer memory, pointing to the path I had left unvisited.

I decided to write stories on the Tibetans, refugees whose worlds intrigued me. I returned to Dharamshala and began meeting older Tibetans, the generation that had seen free Tibet, and were now in the autumn of their lives. Stoic old men and women with weather-beaten faces, rheumy eyes that could still shine with hidden fires when they talked of their homeland. Age had not been able to dim their memories. Holding polished prayer beads, they told tales of their lives with minimal drama. Sometimes a tear would roll down and the dam of memory would breach as they remembered pain, loss, the faces and places where they had laid down their hearts.

I met many young Tibetans too, those born and brought up in India with landscapes different to their grandparents and parents. They were Tibetan to their core, yet they had bits of India in them. They knew Bollywood numbers even before they remembered their own folk songs. Their Hindi was impeccable. Many of them had studied in mainstream Indian schools. Yet integration with India was problematic as they lacked citizenship and their Resident Cards made employment in the corporate world difficult despite educational qualifications. This was one reason so many had gravitated to McLeod Ganj, setting up small businesses as there weren't enough jobs within the Tibetan Government in Exile. The underlying reason of course was their deep wish to support the cause of a Free Tibet. Some restless young folk spoke of Rangzen which means complete freedom in Tibet for Tibetans. Many others wanted to apply for Indian passports, yet others felt it compromised the Tibetan cause.

'One ancient nation is dying,' is how the Dalai Lama often begins his talks, looking for salvation for his people across the world stage as Tibet's 2,100-year-old civilization faces extinction in its homeland. There have been nine rounds of talks between Dharamshala and Beijing, in which the Dalai Lama's initial 1987 Five Point Peace Plan asking the whole of Tibet to be transformed into a demilitarized zone of peace was rejected outright by the Chinese. The Dalai Lama's Middle Way Approach—relinquishing Tibetan independence for secure autonomy—has also failed to elicit any concessions from Beijing. It is as if Beijing waits for the Dalai Lama's passing away to end its 'Tibet problem.' The Tibetans' biggest fear is that their God King may die in exile.

Despite so many setbacks, the Dalai Lama continues to smilingly guide his people, preaching the Buddhist way of peace and non-violence.

In settlements such as Dharamshala and McLeod Ganj, the Tibetan community have rebuilt their lives through toil and difficulty, facing poverty and pain in unfamiliar terrain. The old folk have seen the worst of it but many appear stoic, speaking little of their travails. When I began talking to them, I realized that people never speak the way you want to write about them—they speak compressing years into a few sentences, leave out their feelings, skim over their pain and loss, and leave a lot unsaid—what I got were mere bones.

So I started reading up on the Tibetans, doing research before I began to write their stories—imagining conversations and stitching a life to cover the bones and make a person whole. My initial idea of the stories being part-fiction part-reality remains, but the truth is that the lines have blurred. In the end the stories I tell you are the way I have perceived them and imagined they must have happened. If there are underlying flaws, it is all because of my inability to see through any other prism.

It has been a privilege to bring out small glimpses of lived lives that have seen humanity at its worst and its best, known heartbreaking loss and garnered the spirit to put together a new world. The Tibetan ability to endure and to keep alive their struggle for their homeland is deeply entrenched in their faith and in that lies their salvation.

I thank Lhasang Tsering for the use of the title 'Tibet with My Eyes Closed'. It is the title of a poem that he wrote evoking the vast highland meadows and swirling winds of the lost Tibetan homeland that his people still see in their dreams.

This book would never have happened without the constant support of my husband Shakti who travelled with me to different places to meet Tibetans. Of all the journeys we made the one to Mustang was for both of us a trip of a lifetime—unforgettable. Shakti is the first one to read my drafts, do the edits and tell me if the stories worked. His enthusiastic backing is what made this book possible.

Equally important has been the ready support, guidance and editing of my friend Sujata Madhok.

I want to thank all the people who told their stories—some of their names have been changed for obvious reasons as they have families still living in Tibet but I deeply value their time and sharing.

This book would have never happened without the enormous friendship and open-heartedness of Thupten Samphel, Director of the Tibet Policy Institute. My deep gratitude to Drechen who translated and helped me understand small nuances of Tibetan language and culture. I also want to thank my schoolmate Gompu and his enormous help in every sphere. Also, a big thank you to other school friends Sangay and Tamdin, and above all to Sonam Yangchen Rana for her unstinting support.

If I have told the stories, it is Vikram Singh Verma's sketches of windswept mountain sides, fluttering prayer flags and remote inhospitable terrain that make the book come alive.

My sincere thanks to Ravi Singh of Speaking Tiger, to my friend, guide and literary agent Preeti Gill and finally many thanks to my editor Yauvanika Chopra.

Finally, it may be mere coincidence or just a turn of the cycle of karma—2019 marks sixty years of Tibetans in India—it is also the year I turned sixty.

www.ingramcontent.com/pod-product-compliance
Lightning Source LLC
Chambersburg PA
CBHW052056230426
43662CB00037B/1924